THINK
ABOUT IT!

Also available

Gifted and Talented Education from A–Z
Jacquie Buttriss and Ann Callander
1-84312-256-1

Teaching Thinking Skills Across the Primary Curriculum
A practical approach for all abilities
Belle Wallace (ed.)
1-85346-766-9

Teaching Thinking Skills Across the Middle Years
A practical approach for children aged 9–14
Belle Wallace and Richard Bentley (eds)
1-85346-767-7

Thinking Skills and Problem-solving – an Inclusive Approach
A practical guide for teachers in primary schools
Belle Wallace, June Maker, Diana Cave and Simon Chandler
1-84312-107-7

Using History to Develop Thinking Skills at Key Stage 2
Belle Wallace and Peter Riches
1-85346-928-9

Using Literacy to Develop Thinking Skills with Children Aged 5–7
Paula Iley
1-84312-282-0

Using Literacy to Develop Thinking Skills with Children Aged 7–11
Paula Iley
1-84312-283-9

Using Science to Develop Thinking Skills at Key Stage 1
Practical resources for gifted and talented learners
Max de Boo
1-84312-150-6

Discovering and Developing Talent in Schools
An Inclusive Approach
Bette Gray-Fow
1-84312-669-9

Challenges in Primary Science
Meeting the Needs of Able Young Scientists at Key Stage 2
David Coates and Helen Wilson
1-84312-013-5

THINK ABOUT IT!

Thinking Skills Activities for Years 3 and 4

Jacquie Buttriss • Ann Callander

 David Fulton Publishers

National Association for Able Children in Education

In association with
The National Association for Able Children in Education

David Fulton Publishers Ltd
The Chiswick Centre, 414 Chiswick High Road, London W4 5TF

www.fultonpublishers.co.uk

First published in Great Britain in 2005 by David Fulton Publishers.

10 9 8 7 6 5 4 3 2 1

Note: The right of Jacquie Buttriss and Ann Callander to be identified as the authors of this work has been asserted by them in accordance with the Copyright, Designs and Patents Act 1988.

David Fulton Publishers is a division of Granada Learning Limited, part of ITV plc.

British Library Cataloguing in Publication Data
A catalogue record for this book is available from the British Library.

ISBN 1–84312–234–0

Illustrations by Bridget Dowty
Typeset by FiSH Books, London
Printed and bound in Great Britain by Ashford Colour Press

Contents

NACE National Office
PO Box 242
Arnolds Way
Oxford,
OX2 9FR
Tel: 01865 861879
Fax: 01865 861880

**National Association
for Able Children
in Education**

NACE exists solely to support the daily work of teachers providing for pupils with high ability, whilst enabling all pupils to flourish

We are a large association of professionals. We deliver advice, training and materials on learning and teaching; leadership and management; whole-school improvement.

We provide:
- Specialist advice and information to teachers, LEAs and government agencies
- Courses, some in partnership with Granada Learning Professional Development and with optional online continuing support and access to tutors
- Bespoke courses and guidance delivered at your premises
- Tutors to work alongside teachers in the classroom
- Annual and regional conferences
- Market-leading books and seminal publications
- Keynote speakers for special events
- Support for special projects
- National and international links

Some of our most popular courses are linked to our best-selling books and delivered by the author; an opportunity to really understand new strategies and how to put them into practice.

Join us: membership gives you:
- Quick access to professional advice and resources
- Members' website, for updates and exchange of practice
- Termly newsletters, with practical articles and updates
- Biannual journals with more substantial articles relating research to practical strategies
- Discount on courses and conferences
- Access to network of members and regional groups

**Visit www.nace.co.uk
for list of publications, courses, services and to join NACE**

Advancing teaching: Inspiring able learners every day

Founded in 1984   Registered Charity No. 327230

Introduction

Helping children to be more metacognitive learners (i.e. to become more aware of their own thinking) is a crucial factor in developing effective learners.

(Primary National Strategy, DfES 2004: 12)

Think About It! is a practical, classroom resource for teachers of Years 3 and 4 children. It translates the thinking skills outlined by the Primary National Strategy (DfES 2004) and the National Curriculum (DfES/QCA 2000) into user-friendly lesson plans which develop each of the skills and cover the whole primary school curriculum:

- Enquiry
- Problem solving
- Creative thinking
- Information processing
- Reasoning
- Evaluation.

These six thinking skills are referred to as 'cognitive aspects of learning' in the Primary National Strategy's *Excellence and Enjoyment* materials. Six 'affective aspects of learning' (self-awareness, managing feelings, motivation, empathy, social skills and communication) also have a considerable effect on pupils' acquisition of thinking skills and are developed alongside the thinking skills in *Think About It!* activities.

How to use this book

We have designed all the activities in this book to be used in mixed-ability mainstream classes and they all incorporate teaching ideas to support special educational needs (SEN) children and extension strategies for your most able pupils. We also provide general guidelines for SEN support and extension for able, gifted and talented children, which you can adapt to suit any lesson, as well as suggestions for teacher and self-assessment.

Each *Think About It!* activity has a structured lesson plan, with differentiation built in, linked to a number of curriculum areas. Thinking skills and curriculum links are identified for each lesson on its own coverage indicator, and the matrix of coverage gives an overview for all the activities. Activities are grouped into three term units with increasing levels of challenge and can be taken in any order. Lesson plans comprise a range of multi-sensory learning strategies to give all children the opportunity to use their learning strengths in order to develop and extend new skills.

Individual thinking frameworks have been produced as 'Thinking Books' which set out the National Curriculum thinking skills in child-friendly language for use during each lesson. It is very important to give children time for reflection at appropriate intervals, both during tasks and as part of the self-review process. These Thinking Books aim to help children to reflect on the thinking and learning strategies they have used in *Think About It!* activities and in other lessons across the curriculum. There is also a self-assessment sheet entitled 'How am I doing?' for them to use either as part of their Thinking Books, or to identify their strengths and review their progress over time.

All children need to be given opportunities to transfer and generalise the skills they learn in order to ensure that these skills remain in their long-term memory. We have therefore included specific teaching for transfer within each lesson plan, as well as suggesting a range of cross-curricular teaching links as additional opportunities for transferring and practising skills in other learning situations.

This book has been written mainly for class teachers of mixed-ability Years 3 and 4 classes. It is intended for flexible use, which might include using *Think About It!* activities as:

- a focus for the explicit teaching of one or more of the thinking skills
- starting points before extending skills and strategies in other curriculum areas
- part of a series of lessons relating to key skills and specific areas of the curriculum
- a focus for developing children's ability to become metacognitive learners (helping them to think about the skills they are using for thinking and learning).

The following sections provide specific explanations and support to help you make optimum use of *Think About It!* activities in your classroom and to involve your pupils as actively as possible in developing an understanding of their own thinking and learning.

Key thinking skills – cognitive aspects of learning

The National Curriculum defines problem solving as a 'key skill', together with five specific 'thinking skills', all of which are identified as 'cognitive aspects of learning' in the Primary National Strategy's *Excellence and Enjoyment* professional development materials (2004).

Enquiry

Enquiry skills enable pupils to ask relevant questions, to pose and define problems, to plan what to do and how to research, to predict outcomes and anticipate consequences, and to test conclusions and improve ideas.

Problem solving

Problem solving includes the skills of identifying and understanding the problem, ways to solve a problem, monitoring progress in tackling a problem and reviewing a solution to a problem.

Creative thinking

Creative thinking skills enable pupils to generate and extend ideas, to suggest hypotheses, to apply imagination, and to look for alternative innovative outcomes.

Information processing

Information processing skills enable pupils to locate and collect relevant information, to sort, classify, sequence, compare and contrast, and to analyse part/whole relationships.

Reasoning

Reasoning skills enable pupils to give reasons for opinions and actions, to draw inferences and make deductions, to use precise language to explain what they think, and to make judgements and decisions informed by reasons or evidence.

Evaluation

Evaluation skills enable pupils to evaluate information, to judge the value of what they read, hear or do, to develop criteria for judging the value of their own and others' work or ideas, and to have confidence in their judgements.

Lesson format

Learning objectives: (main thinking skills to be developed/practised)

Connect and prepare (whole class)

It is important to establish what pupils know already in order to help them make connections between previous experiences and new areas of their learning. The children then need to be prepared for the task. The activities in this part of the lesson should act as a bridge between the knowledge and skills already gained and the knowledge and skills to be learned.

Think, do, review

Think – (individual) Pupils may need to be given the opportunity to think about the activity individually before they are given the opportunity to explore, clarify and define the task with a partner or small group.

Do – (pairs or small groups) Where possible, the task should involve multi-sensory experiences. Teachers can encourage children to use their strengths while, at the same time, supporting any learning difficulties. While pupils are completing the task, it will be helpful for the teacher (and other adults) to visit groups and prompt them with open-ended questions to stimulate discussion.

Review – (small groups) Time to review and evaluate the thinking processes used during a task as well as the quality of the outcomes.

Transfer and compare (whole class or small groups)

This part of the lesson allows pupils to review the activity and transfer the knowledge and skills they have learned to another task. They can:

- share and compare their ideas
- explore variation
- justify and evaluate the different alternatives.

Thinking about thinking (individual)

This is where pupils can be helped to reflect on the thinking skills and strategies they have used to complete their tasks and how well they are developing metacognitive strategies to support their learning.

Think-links

Pupils should be encouraged to link these thinking skills activities to the school curriculum and to their everyday life. They should be able to explore ways in which they might use specific thinking skills in a variety of situations.

Specific support for SEN and extension for able, gifted and talented pupils

Where there is advice relating to the specific activity for supporting SEN pupils or for extension for able, gifted and talented pupils this is given in italics as 'SEN support' and 'Extension', respectively, and marked with an arrow symbol (⇨). More general advice for supporting these pupils is given in the next section.

Support for SEN children (general advice)

The following advice should allow for the successful inclusion of most SEN pupils in the *Think About It!* activities. However, there may be children with more specific learning difficulties who may need more individual support than is suggested either here or in the individual lesson plans. Generally SEN children will need support with:

- understanding key concept vocabulary
- reading information
- expressing ideas in group discussion
- recording ideas and information
- contributing to class discussion and feedback.

Understanding key concept vocabulary

1. Provide visual cues to remind children of word and phrase meanings. Visual cues could be pictures, symbols, diagrams, maps, charts or posters.

2. Provide concrete materials and practical experiences to help children consolidate their understanding of key concept vocabulary.

Reading information

1. Pair a more able reader with a less able reader or ensure that there are one or two more able readers in a group to lead the reading part of the activity.

2. Provide adult support for the reading part of the activity (teacher or teaching assistant).

3. Allow children to listen to an audio-taped version of the text.

Expressing ideas in group discussion

1. Pause – allow children individual thinking time before asking them to talk to a partner about their ideas.

2. Prompt – use open-ended questions during activities and encourage children to give fuller explanations by prompting them to give reasons for their answers.

3. Praise – give positive feedback where possible.

Recording ideas and information

1. Allow children to use alternative methods of recording (labelled pictures, comic strips, diagrams, charts, maps, writing frames, ICT programmes).

2. Allow children to show their ideas through mime, role play, practical demonstrations and talks.

3. Allow children to use audio tapes to record their ideas.

Contributing to class discussion and feedback

1. Use a range of different types and levels of questioning in order to give all children opportunities to take part.

2. Encourage children to ask each other questions during feedback sessions.

3. Allow children to use concrete materials and visual aids when offering feedback.

Extension for able, gifted and talented children (general advice)

Extension (also referred to as enrichment in depth), involves children and young people following the standard curriculum but developing a deeper understanding through encountering more complex resources and materials, tackling more challenging questions and tasks, demonstrating higher levels of thinking, and presenting increasingly sophisticated responses.

[QCA Guidance on teaching the gifted and talented – Managing Provision – www.nc.uk.net/gt]

Involving gifted and talented children in developing a deeper understanding means ensuring that tasks are differentiated for level, pace, complexity and depth. Use strategies such as:

- build complexity into whole-class activities (e.g. more complex investigations and problem-solving activities)
- access the main learning objective(s) at a deeper level
- apply learning objectives in less familiar contexts
- challenge children's thinking with more abstract ideas and concepts
- specify more demanding criteria
- provide access to more demanding materials and resources
- encourage independence in planning tasks, organising approaches and presenting findings
- encourage children to extend ideas of their own
- use higher order questioning to stimulate a greater depth of thought and understanding
- probe or challenge answers and assumptions to deepen children's thinking
- challenge children to make their understanding more explicit
- encourage children to reflect on and evaluate at greater depth on what they have achieved
- develop a community of enquiry where pupils can begin to ask, investigate and answer questions together.

Skilful questioning, within the classroom, can be key to help children to develop their thinking skills. Asking different types of questions can extend tasks in different ways. Such questions might focus on:

- attention (What did you notice?)
- enquiry (How can we find out?)
- comparison (How often? How long?)
- viewpoint (Can you explain from another point of view?)
- investigation (What if…?)
- clarification (Can you explain what you mean?)
- reasoning (Can you give reasons for your answer?)
- application (What other examples can you think of?)
- synthesis (How could we add to or improve…?)
- evaluation (What do you think about…? What are your criteria?)
- philosophical (What is happiness?).

When asking questions, it is important to give pupils appropriate opportunities to reflect before giving their answers (and in the evaluation of those answers).

Assessment

The 'Assessment for Learning' initiative has given teachers an extensive range of everyday strategies for formatively assessing pupils' learning. Many of these strategies are particularly effective in assessing thinking skills across the curriculum. In *Think About It!* each lesson plan includes opportunities for reflection, transfer and review of thinking and learning. Helping pupils to transfer and apply their learning in new contexts develops their higher-order thinking skills. By building in transfer activities in every lesson and suggesting further, cross-curricular 'think-links', pupils are encouraged to gain confidence in transferring learned thinking skills to new situations, which in turn creates secure foundations for subsequent learning. Assessment of how well pupils transfer their learning is therefore a very effective guide to their thinking skills progress.

One of the key principles of *Think About It!* is that of making pupils active partners in their learning by encouraging them to think about how they think and learn. An important aspect of this is the encouragement of pupils' reflection on their progress through thinking time, discussion, self-assessment and review.

Thinking Books prompt pupils to identify, discuss and record which thinking skills they have used in each lesson, through a range of child-friendly statements. The last page of the Thinking Books is a self-assessment page which can be used at any stage of the process, either at the end of an individual lesson, or at the end of a module, term or year.

In the Primary National Strategy's (DfES 2004) *Excellence and Enjoyment: Learning and teaching in the primary years* module entitled 'Learning to learn: progression in key aspects of learning', each of the thinking skills is outlined (using the National Curriculum 2000 framework) and illustrated through a very useful list of assessment indicators. These indicators provide an excellent framework for the assessment of thinking skills.

Everyday strategies for assessing pupils' progress in thinking skills in *Think About It!* lessons across the curriculum, might include:

- observation
- listening to pupils' discussions
- open-ended questioning (giving pupils time to think before answering)
- probing to assess the extent and depth of thinking
- review-checks to assess understanding and progress
- peer-assessments – supporting pupils to assess progress/outcomes in pairs/groups
- pupils' own self-assessments (either orally or in their Thinking Books).

Applying these strategies to the assessment indicators for each thinking skill, using either the *Excellence and Enjoyment* model or the child-friendly statements set out in pupils' individual Thinking Books, will enable you to adapt and extend learning opportunities appropriately for each child.

Matrix of coverage

The *Think About It!* matrix of coverage (Table 1.1) is designed to show, at a glance, which subjects and thinking skills are addressed by each activity. The symbols used are full (black) or empty circles to show main or subordinate coverage of subject areas, respectively. All thinking skills used in activities are indicated by full circles.

Coverage indicators on lesson plans

At the side of each lesson plan is a diagram or coverage grid that indicates the curriculum areas and thinking skills covered by the activity. For example:

Curriculum coverage

Ly	●
Ny	
Sc	
ICT	
RE	
Hi	>
Gg	>
DT	
AD	
Mu	
PE	○
PSHE	●

Thinking skills

Enqu	
Prob	
Crea	●
Info	
Reas	●
Eval	●

The abbreviations used are:
Curriculum coverage: Ly, literacy; Ny, numeracy; Sc, science; ICT, information and communications technology; RE, religious education; Hi, history; Gg, geography; DT, design technology; AD, art and design; Mu, music; PE, physical education; PSHE, personal, social and health education.
Thinking skills: Enqu, enquiry; Prob, problem solving; Crea, creative thinking; Info, information processing; Reas, reasoning; Eval, evaluation.

The symbols used are:

Curriculum coverage

- ● Main curriculum areas covered
- ○ Subsidiary curriculum areas covered
- > Think-links – transferring skills across additional curriculum areas

Thinking skills

- ● Main thinking skills used.

Table 1.1 Think About It!

Matrix of coverage of subject areas and thinking skills

Activity	Subjects[a]												Thinking skills[b]					
	Ly	Ny	Sc	ICT	RE	Hi	Gg	DT	Mu	AD	PE	PSHE	Enqu	Prob	Crea	Info	Reas	Eval
Section 1																		
Black and White Animals	○	●														●	●	
Ben's Team	●		●								○	●			●	●	●	●
Celebrations	○	●			●										●		●	
The Talkative Tortoise	●									●					●		●	
Market Day	○	●												●	●			
Invent a Sport	○	○									●	●	●		●			●
Either...Or...	●											●			●		●	
What Number Am I?	○	●															●	
Who Should be King?	●				○							●		●			●	●
Rhythm and Movement	●								●						●			
The Romans are Coming!	○					●									●	●	●	
Christmas Crackers		●												●	●	●		
Section 2																		
Snakes and Lizards	○		●				●						●	●	●	●	●	●
Lost!						●	●							●	●	●		
Noah's Ark	○	○			●	●									●	●		
Once Upon a Time	●	●		○		●							●			●		
Plague Village!	○		○	○				○				○			●			
Something to Drink	●		○				●	●						●	●			●
What If?	○			●			●	●			●			●	●	●		●
Making Music									●							●		
Toys and Games		○				●	●								●	●		
Decisions and Consequences	●						●					●			●		●	●
End Product	●							●		●								
Playground Problems	●						●					●		●		●		●
Section 3																		
Pirates!		●				●										●		
Fossil Hunter	●	●				●									●	●	●	
Roman Numbers		●				●										●	●	
Eating Habits			●								●					●		
Yes or No?		●	○										●			●		
The Yeti – Does it Exist?	●		○	○		○	○					○			●	●	●	
A Week at School		●								○		○				●		
Promises	●					●						●	●		●			●
Family Tree	○									●	●	○			●		●	
Sports Day	●							●			●			●	●	●	●	●
The Challenge of King Minos		●														●		
Holiday Races																		
Totals (coverage)	24	14	6	3	3	8	5	4	2	3	4	11	6	9	17	15	14	9

[a] Ly, literacy; Ny, numeracy; Sc, science; ICT, information and communications technology; RE, religious education; Hi, history; Gg, geography; DT, design technology; AD, art and design; Mu, music; PE, physical education; PSHE, personal, social and health education.

[b] Enqu, enquiry; Prob, problem solving; Crea, creative thinking; Info, information processing; Reas, reasoning; Eval, evaluation.

● main coverage of subject area; ○ subsidiary coverage of subject area.

CHAPTER 2

Individual thinking frameworks – Thinking Books

What are Thinking Books?

When the mind is thinking it is talking to itself.

(Plato)

When we listen to ourselves thinking we are using metacognitive strategies; that is, we are becoming aware of the thinking skills and processes that we are using in order to complete a task. Metacognitive strategies include:

- making connections between prior knowledge and new concepts and linking ideas
- consciously selecting the most suitable thinking skills for a task and being able to give clear explanations on how these skills are used
- reviewing and evaluating the thinking skills and processes used during a task
- transferring thinking skills and processes to other tasks both across the curriculum and in everyday situations.

Children often have difficulty in responding when asked to explain how they solved a problem or planned an investigation because they are not aware of the skills and strategies they have used during the task. The 'Thinking Books' are designed to raise children's awareness of their own thinking processes by expecting them to:

- identify the thinking skills they have used in specific activities
- recognise when they have transferred these skills to other activities across the curriculum and in everyday situations
- assess how well they can use these skills in different situations.

What is important here is that children are encouraged and supported to think about how they have approached tasks and developed their learning. Thinking Books are intended to help this process. However, if teachers choose not to use Thinking Books as individual records for the children to use, they can nonetheless be helpful as a guide to what thinking skills pupils have used, expressed in child-friendly language that they can readily understand.

The child-friendly statements have been adapted directly from the National Curriculum and aim to help children reflect on the thinking and learning strategies they have used to complete *Think About It!* activities and in other curriculum lessons.

We have included the appropriate concept vocabulary under each child-friendly statement in order to help children to develop an understanding of the key terminology for the various thinking processes.

How to use Thinking Books

Thinking Books are designed to be photocopied and stapled for each child's ongoing use. They are intended to be individual frameworks for the children themselves to use to record what thinking skills they have used; how and when they have used them.

You may want to adapt Thinking Books to use in your own preferred way, but one approach we have successfully trialled is to give pupils a few minutes at the end of each lesson to identify and record (either as a class, in groups, pairs or individually) which skills they have used in this activity. The easiest way for them to do this is to simply write the name of the activity (e.g. 'Black and White Animals') in the space next to the aspect of a thinking skill that they think they used most. Alternatively, you may prefer to give your children exercise books to use as a narrative to reflect on the development of their thinking and learning.

In the Thinking Book included here there is one page for each of the six key thinking skills, plus a self-assessment sheet entitled 'How am I doing?' which can be used separately, at the end of term perhaps, for the children to assess their strengths and progress over time. This sheet could easily be incorporated, perhaps as an end page, in pupils' Thinking Books.

NAME .... YEAR ....

Thinking Book

Think About It!

Individual Thinking Frameworks

Enquiry skills

Skills I have used	*Think About It!* activities in which I used these skills	Other lessons in which I used these skills
I can ask questions that lead to useful answers. *(Ask relevant questions)*		
I can set and explain problems clearly. *(Pose and define problems)*		
I can plan what to do and how to find the information I need. *(Plan research)*		
I can say what I think will happen at the end of an activity. *(Predict outcomes; anticipate consequences)*		
I can think about whether results or decisions seem correct and whether there might have been a better way. *(Test conclusions; improve ideas)*		

Problem solving skills

Skills I have used	*Think About It!* activities in which I used these skills	Other lessons in which I used these skills
I can see and understand what the problem is. *(Identify and understand the problem)*		
I can plan the things I need to do to try and solve the problem. *(Plan how to solve the problem)*		
I can think about how I'm doing, considering a range of possible solutions. *(Monitor progress in tackling the problem)*		
I can review how well my chosen solutions work, or what else I might need to do. *(Review the solution to the problem)*		

Creative thinking skills

Skills I have used	*Think About It!* activities in which I used these skills	Other lessons in which I used these skills
I can think up ideas and then add to them. *(Think up and extend ideas)*		
I can use my imagination to help make my ideas better. *(Apply imagination)*		
I can suggest explanations about why something is the way it is. *(Suggest hypotheses)*		
I can look for other, new ways of doing things. *(Find alternative, innovative outcomes)*		

Information processing skills

Skills I have used	*Think About It!* activities in which I used these skills	Other lessons in which I used these skills
I can find the information I need. *(Locate and collect)*		
I can sort information into different sets. *(Sort, match and classify)*		
I can put information in the right order. *(Sequence)*		
I can see what information is similar and what is different. *(Compare)*		
I can see how different parts of information are related and how they fit together. *(Analyse patterns and relationships)*		

Reasoning skills

Skills I have used	*Think About It!* activities in which I used these skills	Other lessons in which I used these skills
I can give reasons for the things I think and do. *(Give reasons for opinions and actions)*		
I can think about information to work out what it means. *(Draw inference; make deductions)*		
I can use appropriate words to explain what I think. *(Give clear explanations)*		
I can use all the evidence I have to make up my mind. *(Make judgements)*		

Evaluation skills

Skills I have used	*Think About It!* activities in which I used these skills	Other lessons in which I used these skills
I can decide how useful or important information is. *(Evaluate information)*		
I can think up ways to help me to judge the value of my own and others' ideas. *(Develop criteria for judging value of ideas)*		
I feel confident about the decisions I make. *(Have confidence in own judgements)*		

Self-assessment Sheet

Thinking about thinking – How am I doing?

I learn best when I….				
I like to solve problems by….				
I like finding out information by….				
The kind of thinking I'm best at is…. because….				
The kind of thinking I find most difficult is…. because….				
My thinking skills target is….				

CHAPTER 3

Activities – Term 1

This chapter includes lesson plans and activity sheets for the following *Think About It!* activities.

Black and White Animals

A Carroll diagram

One of the most famous children's writers, Lewis Carroll, invented a diagram to help him sort out his ideas.

Here is a Carroll diagram for black and white animals.

	Can fly	Can't fly
Lays eggs		
Doesn't lay eggs		

Put these animals where you think they belong in the Carroll diagram:

panda ostrich dog magpie penguin
badger zebra cat

_____

Now think of a different idea and make up your own Carroll diagram with a partner. Try it out and make sure it works.

Black and White Animals

Curriculum coverage

Ly	○
Ny	●
Sc	●
ICT	
RE	
Hi	>
Gg	>
DT	
AD	>
Mu	>
PE	>
PSHE	

Main learning objective: to sort and classify information, giving reasons for their choices.

Connect and prepare

1. Ask pupils if they can think of a famous children's author who wrote a book about a child who changed size. Then show them a copy of *Alice in Wonderland* and tell them about Lewis Carroll and his interest in logic and maths problems.

2. Talk about sorting and classifying using a Carroll diagram. Draw a blank grid on the board and ask pupils how they think this might be used. (Give them some thinking time.) Then put in some headings and ask them again. Now complete a blank grid together as a whole class. This could be quite simple (for example, shapes with four sides/not with four sides and 2D shapes/not 2D shapes). Ask pupils to suggest other topics they could classify in this way.

Thinking skills

Enqu	
Prob	
Crea	
Info	●
Reas	
Eval	

Think, do, review

Hand out copies of the activity sheet.

Think – Ask pupils to read and think about the first task on the activity sheet, then tell you or each other what they will need to do.

⇨ *SEN support: Assist these pupils with reading and prompt their discussion.*

Do – Complete the first task in pairs. (Ask pupils to suggest additional animals.)

⇨ *Extension: Ask able pupils to work out the fraction or percentage of animals in each sector (without using calculators!).*

Review – Ask pairs to share their solutions with each other, giving reasons for their choices.

Transfer and compare

- Complete the second task on the activity sheet in pairs (thinking of their own headings and items).

  ⇨ *SEN support: SEN pupils may need help to get them started.*

  ⇨ *Extension: Able pupils could draw and use their own Carroll diagram with more rows and columns (at least three of each) – how will this work?*

- As a group/class, share and compare the different choices children have made, asking some of them to explain what they chose to do, why and how well it worked out.

Thinking about thinking

Help pupils to assess the thinking skills they have used in this activity and, if time allows, record them in their Thinking Books.

Think-links

Help children to identify other areas of the curriculum where you might use Carroll diagrams for sorting and classifying information, such as:

Literacy – to identify attributes of different characters in a story or features of a genre;

History – to identify aspects of different historical events or characters;

Geography – to differentiate between a range of conditions, features or locations;

Music – to recognise the features of a range of composers, styles or instruments;

Art and design – to identify elements of a range of media, artists or styles;

PE – to note differences between a variety of sports or other activities.

Ben's Team

Ben's team	Jack's team
I	want
to	be
on	Ben's
team.	I
want	to
win	the
game.	But
when	it's
time	for
Ben	to
pick	he
never	calls
my	name.

Now answer these questions, giving reasons for your answers.

(a) How did you feel when you read this poem?

(b) How do you think Ben and Jack each felt?

(c) Do you think that Ben and Jack had been allowed to pick teams before?

(d) Can you think of any other way of deciding which children should be in each team?

Thinking skills

Enqu	
Prob	
Crea	●
Info	
Reas	●
Eval	●

Ben's Team

Main learning objectives: express own views and opinions; give reasons for ideas, using evidence from the text; consider different points of view.

Connect and prepare

1. Discuss what makes a good team. List attributes needed to be a good team member.

2. Hand out copies of the activity sheet. Read the poem aloud to the class and give children time to discuss the questions.

Think, do, review

Think – Ask children to look again at the way the poem is set out and consider possible clues this gives about the situation.

Do – Ask children, in small groups to discuss:
   – The person who wrote this poem wanted to join one of the teams. Which team do you think he wanted to join?
   – Which team do you think he joined? How do you know?

Give reasons for your answers using evidence from the poem.

⇨ *SEN support: Adult to prompt SEN pupils by asking them about their experiences of being 'left out'. Encourage them to think of ways of overcoming these problems.*

⇨ *Extension: List other situations when children might be made to feel 'left out'.*

Review – As a class, compare the children's ideas, explaining how these are supported by the evidence found in the poem.

Transfer and compare

● As a class have a discussion about different sports that are played in teams. Talk about and list the main skills required for each sport and ask the children to think about the dilemma faced by the captain when picking players for the team.

   ⇨ *SEN support: Assist these pupils by scribing their ideas.*

   ⇨ *Extension: Challenge able pupils to design a grid to classify the main skills of different sports.*

● Ask children to consider the following questions:
   – In team sports do we always need to play to win?
   – How can we ensure that no-one feels left out?

Thinking about thinking

Help pupils to assess the thinking skills they have used in this activity and, if time allows, record them in their Thinking Books.

Think-links

Encourage children to transfer the thinking skills they have used in this activity to other curriculum areas. These could include:

Literacy – use textual evidence to identify different characters' opinions/points of view;

Geography – use environmental evidence to support different views and opinions or use opinion surveys to inform decisions about projects;

History – use primary and secondary sources (artefacts, paintings, photographs, writings) as evidence to support reasoning and to draw conclusions.

Celebrations

How do people in your group celebrate their birthdays?

With a partner, choose four things you do on your birthday (try to choose some unusual things that nobody else does) and write them down in the bar chart below underneath the one that is already written in for you, ('making a wish when you cut the cake'). Now colour in the squares across each line to show how many people in your group do each activity.

Birthdays bar chart

Features of birthdays	Number of people							
	1	2	3	4	5	6	7	8
Making a wish when you cut the cake.								

Celebrations

Curriculum coverage

Ly	○
Ny	●
Sc	>
ICT	
RE	●
Hi	>
Gg	>
DT	>
AD	
Mu	
PE	
PSHE	

Main learning objective: To identify and record similarities and differences in the way people celebrate special occasions.

Connect and prepare

1. Ask children whether they think everyone celebrates birthdays in the same way.
2. Find out who in the class had the most recent birthday. Ask that pupil to come out and describe how he or she celebrated it. Ask other children to put up their hands if they did something different for their birthday (but don't ask them to say what just yet!)

Think, do, review

Thinking skills

Enqu	
Prob	
Crea	
Info	●
Reas	●
Eval	

Think – Tell the class you are going to time them for just 20 seconds, in which you want them to think by closing their eyes and trying to picture in their minds the birthdays they have celebrated recently for different people in their families.

Do – Play a word association game in small groups. Ask the children in their groups to take it in turns around the group, each saying a word to do with birthdays. They should keep going until they run out of ideas. If there is an adult present, or a fluent writer, it may be helpful to have these words written down. (Alternatively, this could be done as a class and listed on the board.)

Review – Discuss as a group the things that people do that are the same (such as giving presents) and the things they do differently (such as having an outing or a party) and emphasise that all have equal validity.

Transfer and compare

Hand out copies of the activity sheet.

● Working in pairs, ask pupils to choose four other features of birthdays (encourage them to choose features not experienced by everyone in the group, such as being measured, or having Grandma to stay) and to use these features to complete the bar chart on the activity sheet.

⇨ *SEN support: SEN pupils to do this as a whole-group activity, led by an adult.*

⇨ *Extension: Challenge more able pupils to find out about birthday customs in other cultures (from books or the Internet) and to report back to the rest of the class at the end of the lesson. (For example, what is different about birthdays in China?)*

● Ask children to show and share their bar charts with other pairs or the whole class and talk about what they have found out.

Thinking about thinking

Help pupils to assess the thinking skills they have used in this activity and, if time allows, record them in their Thinking Books.

Think-links

Encourage pupils to think of other subjects where they could consider similarities and differences, such as:

Science – between animals within groups (e.g. the attributes of different 'big cats');

DT – in the properties of materials (e.g. the stickiness of types of glue);

History – in points of view about historical characters or events;

Geography – features of life in different climates or regions.

The Talkative Tortoise

Beside a pond, in the shade of some trees, there lived a tortoise. Huge water lilies floated on the surface of the pond and wild flowers grew around the edge. Now the tortoise was very happy living by such a beautiful pond but there was only one thing that he longed for and that was a friend. You see the tortoise liked to talk but none of the creatures who lived around the pond had time to talk to him.

One day two wild ducks flew down to look at the pond. They decided to make their home among the bulrushes and began to build a nest. The tortoise was delighted.

'Now I will have someone to talk to,' he said. For several years the tortoise and the ducks lived happily together beside the pond. The tortoise talked and talked and the ducks listened. When they grew tired of listening they flew across the fields and over the hill to a farm where they relaxed by the farmyard pond before returning home in the evening.

One hot summer morning the tortoise went to talk to the ducks. He found them deep in conversation about the level of water in the pond. Sadly they told the tortoise that they could no longer live beside the pond if the rain did not come soon. The tortoise looked up at the sky each morning but no clouds appeared.

At last the ducks decided to fly to the farmyard pond where they knew that the farmer replaced the water each week.

The tortoise begged the ducks to take him with them to their new home.

'But tortoises cannot fly and you could never make the long journey on foot,' they explained.

But the tortoise begged and begged until the ducks felt sorry for him. They agreed to take him with them on one condition. He must not talk at all during the journey. They explained that they could carry the tortoise with them if they each held the end of a strong stick in their beaks and the tortoise held on firmly, by his mouth, in the middle.

The next day the ducks set off with the tortoise holding on firmly to the middle of the stick. They flew across fields and over the hill on the other side of the village.

The tortoise was very excited and wanted to tell the ducks how he felt but he kept quiet. They began to fly lower as they got nearer to the farm. Just as they were passing the village school some children looked up and saw the tortoise. They began to laugh and make fun of the flying tortoise. The tortoise felt very angry inside and opened his mouth to say...

Thinking skills

Enqu	
Prob	
Crea	●
Info	
Reas	●
Eval	

The Talkative Tortoise

Main learning objectives: to predict and anticipate events in a story, give reasons for own ideas and use imagination to create new ideas.

Connect and prepare

1. Working together as a class ask the children if any of them have ever been called chatterboxes and if so why do they think that word has been used to describe them.

2. A wise man called Solomon once said that there is a time for talking and a time for listening – ask pupils if they agree with Solomon.

3. Ask them to suggest some examples of when it is good to talk and when it is good to listen.

Think, do, review

Think – Using the activity sheet tell the children the tale of 'The Talkative Tortoise', using visual aids if possible. This is only the first part of the story so ask the children to think about possible endings. Explain that endings of stories can be happy, sad or funny.

⇨ *Extension: Ask able children to think about what other kinds of story endings there are?*

Do – Ask the children to draw their predictions.

⇨ *Extension: Encourage able children to write an additional explanation about their predictions.*

Review – Ask pupils, as a class or in pairs/groups, to share and review their ideas, giving brief explanations.

Transfer and compare

- Ask the children to design the perfect pond for the tortoise and the ducks, taking into consideration their personalities and likes and dislikes.

- Compare the skills used for designing the perfect pond with those used for drawing predictions about the ending of the story.

Thinking about thinking

Help pupils to assess the thinking skills they have used in this activity and, if time allows, record them in their Thinking Books.

Think-links

Encourage the children to transfer the thinking skills they have used in this activity to other prediction activities. These could include:

Numeracy – estimating measurements, then checking results against estimates;

Science – predicting results of experiments and testing conclusions;

DT – anticipating design problems and experimenting with alternative ideas.

Market Day

Three farmers went to market to buy some new animals.

Sam wanted to buy 20 sheep and 2 cows.
Ash wanted to buy 50 hens and 5 sheep.
Joe wanted to buy 10 hens and 20 cows.

A horse escaped and there was a traffic-jam on the road to the market, so all three farmers arrived late. When they got there, the only animals left on sale were:

10 sheep
20 hens
5 cows.

The three farmers were all friends and they didn't want to argue. They wanted to think of a fair solution to this problem. What do you think they should do?

Ly	○
Ny	●
Sc	
ICT	>
RE	>
Hi	
Gg	>
DT	>
AD	
Mu	
PE	>
PSHE	>

Thinking skills

Enqu	
Prob	●
Crea	●
Info	
Reas	
Eval	

Market Day

Main learning objective: To think creatively in order to solve an open-ended problem.

Connect and prepare

1. Ask pupils to think about the kinds of animals farmers have. Initiate a class discussion about where farmers get their animals from, what a market is like, etc.

2. If any of the children have a difficult problem to solve, how do they work out what to do? (Encourage them to discuss whether, for example, they try to sort it out on their own, or whether they find it helpful to find out more, or to ask other people what they think, or make a list of all the factors.)

Think, do, review

Think – Ask the children to think about what they would do if they and their best friend both wanted to buy something, such as a new DVD or computer game, but there was only one left in the shop. (Give them thinking time before eliciting their ideas.)

Do – Ask the pupils to discuss what they think they would do with a partner, then write down possible solutions and decide which they think would be the best (and why).

Review – Now ask for suggested solutions across the class and discuss the advantages and disadvantages of each option. Are there any unusual or creative solutions? (What about if it was something like a set of stickers or cards – would that have been an easier problem to solve?)

Transfer and compare

● Now give the pupils the Market Day activity sheet and ask them to read through the problem together in pairs or small groups.

⇨ *SEN support: Help SEN pupils with reading the problem or allow them to listen to it on tape.*

● Give everyone some quiet thinking time (to re-read and reflect on the problem), then ask them to suggest some ideas, discuss and reach a pair or group decision. Encourage them to think as creatively and to list all their options.

⇨ *Extension: Suggest that the most able pupils might like to add in complicating factors, such as breeds or ages of animals, or how to get them to the farms.*

- As a whole class, share and compare the options and solutions and how pairs/groups arrived at their final decisions. Help them to evaluate the effectiveness of their solutions and ask whether any groups would want to change them after discussion.

Thinking about thinking

Help pupils to assess the thinking skills they have used in this activity and, if time allows, record them in their Thinking Books.

Think-links

Encourage pupils to make further use of these creative thinking skills for solving open-ended problems and making decisions in other subject areas, such as:

Geography – think about an environmental problem or a local project;

ICT – use computer simulations to explore and solve problems;

RE – consider the decisions people make as a result of their beliefs;

DT – work out how to join materials, or how to make moving joints;

PE – think about how to set out and use gymnastics apparatus;

PSHE – address problems related to pupils' everyday lives at school.

Invent a Sport

Factors to consider

- Will it be a ball sport? (If so, what shaped ball? Only one ball? How will it be moved?)

- Will it be played by teams, pairs or individuals?

- Will it be indoors or outside?

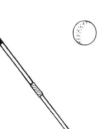

- Will it need a field, court, course or arena? (If so, will it need special markings?)

- Will it need the use of anything mechanical?

- Do you want players to wear special outfits?

- Will they need protective clothing?

- How long will a match or event last?

- What will teams have to do to take the lead or to win?

- What rules will be needed?

- How will people know how it is going, what the score is or who has won?

- Will there be an award or a prize for the winner(s)?

Invent a Sport

Curriculum coverage

Ly	○
Ny	○
Sc	
ICT	
RE	
Hi	
Gg	>
DT	>
AD	>
Mu	>
PE	●
PSHE	●

Thinking skills

Enqu	●
Prob	
Crea	●
Info	
Reas	
Eval	●

Main learning objective: to consider a range of factors and make choices in order to devise and evaluate a new sport.

Connect and prepare

1. Ask for a show of hands – how many children like playing sports or games? Ask for favourite sports and why they like them best. List these on the board.

2. Now ask pupils to brainstorm all the other sports they can think of and add them to the list on the board.

3. Encourage the class to choose symbols to help you classify these sports on the board to identify, for example, those which are ball sports, team sports or indoor sports.

Think, do, review

Think – Pose a question to the class and give them time to think on their own –
– 'What is the difference between a sport and a game?'

Do – Now ask them to discuss in groups what they think are the distinguishing features of sports and games and what is/are the difference(s) between them. They should reach an agreement and write down their decision.

Review – Ask one member of each group to read out their group's decision. Then share and compare these as a class. Ask some further questions:
– 'Is there a clear difference between a game and a sport?'
– 'When is a sport not a game?' or vice versa.
– 'Are all sports competitive?'

Transfer and compare

● Challenge pupils, working in pairs, using the prompts on the activity sheet, to invent a new sport. Draw attention to the range of factors involved (shown by the symbols on your list) and encourage them to consider which of these to select. Ask each pair to agree on some rules and write a brief explanation of the sport and how to play it (or produce a labelled drawing).

⇨ *SEN support: Give SEN pupils some simple guidelines (e.g. a ball sport for two small teams).*

⇨ *Extension: Ask able pupils to imagine they have been watching their new sport and to write the first paragraph of a review for the local newspaper.*

- Ask pairs to gather in groups and tell or read out to each other the description of their new sport. Direct groups to ask questions to each pair to help clarify their thinking about how their sport will work and whether they might need to make any changes.

Thinking about thinking

Help pupils to assess the thinking skills they have used in this task and, if time allows, record them in their Thinking Books.

Think-links

Help children suggest other subject areas where these thinking skills can be used to devise and evaluate, such as:

Geography – invent a leisure activity;

DT – invent a toy;

Art and design – design a three-colour poster;

Music – compose a jingle.

Either...Or...

Here are some statements about situations, together with possible explanations. Each one is an 'either...or...'. Together with a partner, can you think of alternative explanations for the situations?

1. There was a fire engine in the school playground.	Either the school was on fire,	or
2. Katie's birthday party was cancelled.	Either she was ill,	or
3. My mum had to put the crisps back on the supermarket shelf.	Either she didn't have enough money to pay for them,	or
4. The big oak tree fell down.	Either the wind was too strong,	or
5. Sam was woken by the sound of breaking glass	Either a burglar was trying to get into his house,	or
6. Jack had to come off the football field just before half-time.	Either he was sent off by the referee,	or

Either...Or...

Together with a partner, think of six more statements and 'either...or...' explanations of your own to try out on other children in your class to discuss which they think is more likely.

Either...Or...

Curriculum coverage

Ly	●
Ny	>
Sc	
ICT	>
RE	
Hi	>
Gg	
DT	>
AD	
Mu	
PE	
PSHE	●

Main learning objective: to offer alternative explanations for everyday situations and consider their validity.

Connect and prepare

1. Begin the lesson by setting up a situation:

   The teacher heard a bang. She looked up and saw Lucy standing by a broken vase. Either Lucy had knocked the vase off the table or...

2. Ask pupils to suggest possible explanations and discuss their merits or probability.

3. Encourage pupils to recognise that there are often alternative explanations for situations and that we have to make judgements based on the evidence available.

Thinking skills

Enqu	
Prob	
Crea	●
Info	
Reas	●
Eval	

Think, do, review

Hand out copies of activity sheet A.

Think – Ask the pupils to read, either individually or together with you, the explanation on the top of activity sheet A. Can anyone explain in their own words to the rest of the class what they have to do?

Do – The children, working in pairs, should now suggest and discuss together possible options for each of the six situations in order to complete the task on activity sheet A.

⇨ *SEN support: Ask an adult to structure discussions for SEN pupils and scribe their answers or give the pupils a tape recorder to use.*

⇨ *Extension: Ask able pupils to write down at least two alternatives for each statement.*

Review – Ask each pair to share and compare solutions with another pair, giving reasons for their choices.

Transfer and compare

Hand out copies of activity sheet B.

● Ask pupils, working in pairs, to complete the second part of the activity, using activity sheet B to think up their own statements, followed by possible 'either, or' explanations.

⇨ *SEN support: Suggest ideas for statements, so that SEN pupils can concentrate on the 'either, or' parts of the activity.*

⇨ *Extension: Challenge able pupils to think of statements outside their everyday home or school experiences.*

- As pairs or as a class, share and compare some of the statements and explanations children have devised, asking them to evaluate how effectively they have explained their situations and which options they consider to be most likely.

Thinking about thinking

Help pupils to assess the thinking skills they have used in this activity and, if time allows, record them in their Thinking Books.

Think-links

Help the children to identify how they could use this strategy to offer alternative explanations in a range of situations across the curriculum, for example:

Numeracy – alternative solutions to open-ended problems;

History – alternative explanations for historical events, situations or actions;

Geography – alternative explanations for why peoples settled in certain places;

ICT or **DT** – alternative ways of accomplishing a task.

What Number Am I?

Clues	Number
1. I have two digits. My tens digit is an even number. My unit digit is an odd number. The even digit is more than 1 but less than 3. The odd digit is less than 8 but more than 6. My whole number is 3 × 9. What number am I?	
2. I have three digits. One of my digits is the sum of 2 and 4. My hundred digit is more than 7. One of my digits is less than 1. My whole number has no tens and is less than 900. What number am I?	
3. I have four digits. My tens digit is more than 1 but less than 3. One of my digits is an odd number. My units digit can be divided by both 2 and 3. One of my digits is more than 8. My whole number is more than 4000 but less than 5000. What number am I?	
4. I have four digits. My tens digit can be divided by both 2 and 4. All my digits are even numbers. My hundreds digit is half my tens digit. My units digit is half my hundreds digit. My whole number is divisible by two. What number am I?	

Thinking skills

Enqu	
Prob	
Crea	
Info	
Reas	●
Eval	

What Number Am I?

Main learning objective: to analyse written clues in order to make deductions and explain their actions.

Connect and prepare

1. Remind the children of the meaning of the mathematical concept vocabulary used in this activity.

2. Hand out copies of the activity sheet. Work through the first set of clues by working together as a class to make deductions leading to the solution. Talk about the skills and strategies you have all used.

Think, do, review

Think – Remind the children that they need to think carefully about each clue and use different strategies to make their deductions.

Do – Work individually or in pairs to find the numbers for each set of clues.

⇨ *SEN support: Provide visual and concrete cues for maths concept vocabulary. Encourage children to verbalise possible strategies.*

⇨ *Extension: Ask able pupils to make up some clues for numbers of their own choice and record these in the blank spaces on the activity sheet.*

Review – Check answers with another pair and review strategies used.

Transfer and compare

- As a class, listen to some of the clues made up by those children who took part in the extension task. Talk about the skills needed to make up the clues.

- If time allows, build on this discussion to make up clues with the whole class to lead to a number.

- Compare this task of making up clues with the previous task of using clues to work out answers.

Thinking about thinking

Help pupils to assess the thinking skills they have used in this activity and, if time allows, record them in their Thinking Books.

Think-links

Encourage children to transfer the reasoning skills used in this activity to other areas of the curriculum. These could include:

Literacy – writing clues for language games or 'What book/character am I?' clues;

Numeracy – a range of number investigations;

Science – devise 'What am I?' clues for each other to identify animals, plants, materials;

Geography – writing location or 'Where am I?' clues for mapping activities;

History – write 'Who was I?' clues to historical characters.

Who Should be King?

Storyteller: One day the birds had a meeting to choose a new king.

Peacock: The crow is too old to be king.

Magpie: We need a new king.

Eagle: Yes. We need a king who is young and strong.

Storyteller: Now the old crow was wise and kind. He had been the king of the birds for a long time.

Magpie: The crow is a wise bird. We could ask him to help us choose a king.

Peacock: But he might choose a king that we do not like!

Eagle: Then we must choose a king ourselves.

Storyteller: They all looked at each other.

Magpie: A king should be quick and clever.

Eagle: He should be young and strong.

Peacock: He should be tall and handsome.

Storyteller: The eagle and the magpie looked at the peacock.

Magpie: What did you say?

Storyteller: The peacock walked up and down in front of the other birds, showing off his tall tail feathers.

Peacock: I said, the new king should be tall and handsome.

Eagle: Why?

Peacock: He has to look good in royal robes.

Storyteller: The peacock stood still, his feathers shining in the sunlight.

Peacock: A king must look like a king.

Storyteller: The birds all nodded and called for the peacock to be made king.

Eagle: It's true that a king must look like a king. But he must be strong too.

Magpie: Like you, you mean?

Eagle: Yes. Just like me.

Storyteller: The eagle stood straight and tall.

Eagle: I am good-looking but I am also young and strong.

Peacock: Well, you're certainly not shy!

Magpie: Why does a king need to be strong?

Storyteller: The eagle thought for a moment.

Eagle: The king of the birds must be strong enough to win any battle. He must be able to bring back food as well.

Peacock: The old crow always made sure that every bird had enough to eat.

Magpie: Yes. We all need to have food to eat.

Storyteller: The birds all nodded and called for the eagle to be made king.

Magpie: But wait a minute.

Storyteller: The birds turned to look at the magpie.

Magpie: You need to be quick and clever to win a battle.

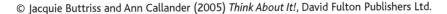

Eagle:	Well. I am clever.
Peacock:	You could have fooled me!
Storyteller:	The magpie hopped on to a rock so that he didn't look so small. He put something down.
Magpie:	Could any of you steal these?
Storyteller:	The birds all looked at the diamonds sparkling in the sunshine.

Eagle:	What's so clever about stealing some shining stones?
Peacock:	They are very pretty stones. They would look good on me.
Magpie:	They are not just stones. If you were as clever as I am you would know that they are jewels for the king's crown.
Storyteller:	The birds all looked at each other and nodded. Then they called for the magpie to be made king.
Peacock:	Wait a minute. Let's think about this. The magpie is not handsome enough.
Eagle:	Or strong enough.
Storyteller:	The birds looked worried. They didn't know what to think.
Peacock:	You need to look good to be a king.
Eagle:	No. A king must be young and strong.
Magpie:	You're both wrong. Being quick and clever is the most important thing.
Storyteller:	The birds could not make up their minds who should be king. What do you think? Could you help them solve their problem?

Words fit for a king

young   strong   quick   clever   wise   tall

powerful   kind   handsome   brave   proud

Who Should be King?

Curriculum coverage

Ly	●
Ny	
Sc	>
ICT	
RE	○
Hi	>
Gg	>
DT	
AD	
Mu	
PE	
PSHE	●

Thinking skills

Enqu	
Prob	●
Crea	
Info	
Reas	●
Eval	●

Main learning objectives: consider a range of possible solutions to a problem, justify opinions and use evidence to support reasoning.

Connect and prepare

1. What is a friend? Ask the class to brainstorm some words that describe what they mean by the word 'friend' (e.g. kind, fun, helpful, caring etc.) and make a list on the board.
2. Ask the children to vote for the word they think is the most important when describing a friend.

Think, do, review

Hand out copies of the activity sheet.

Think – Ask the children to look at the 'Words fit for a king' at the end of the play and think about which one they feel is most important when describing a king.

Do – Ask the children to read the play together in groups of four and talk about which of the characters in the play would make the best king and why. Now encourage them to think beyond the play. In the Old Testament part of the Bible the Israelites wanted a king. They were given a man called Saul. King Saul was tall, handsome, brave, moody and jealous. Ask the children to discuss what sort of a king you think he made and give their reasons why.

⇨ **SEN support:** *Put less able readers in a group with more able readers to support them. Use adult intervention for part of the session, using pause, prompt, praise techniques.*

⇨ **Extension:** *Ask able pupils to think about alternative types of personality for king. Extend thinking into the overall qualities of leadership and the wisdom of relying on one person as a leader, or having different leaders for different situations.*

Review – Ask the children to compare their decisions with each other or the whole class and review the evidence for their thoughts and ideas.

Transfer and compare

Initiate further discussion: Does a leader have to be a king? Who else do children think should be a leader and why? Leader of what? (Encourage them to think of other animals, people they know, famous people – king/queen of pop, football, etc.)

Thinking about thinking

Help pupils to assess the thinking skills they have used in this activity and, if time allows, record them in their Thinking Books.

Think-links

Encourage children to transfer the thinking skills they have used in this activity to identify qualities needed in other situations, such as:

Literacy – qualities suited to characters in stories;

Science – qualities needed by scientists and researchers;

History – qualities needed in different roles in history, not just kings and queens;

Geography – qualities needed by explorers;

RE – desirable qualities for religious leaders;

PSHE – qualities suited to taking responsibilities at school, at home and in other everyday situations.

Rhythm and Movement

Curriculum coverage

Ly		
Ny	●	
Sc		
ICT	>	
RE		
Hi		
Gg		
DT		
AD	>	
Mu	●	
PE	>	
PSHE		

Main learning objective: to use imagination when responding to stimuli and try out alternative ideas.

Connect and prepare

1. As a class, ask the children to listen to and then join in a repeated, clapped rhythm.
2. Change the rhythm and tap with your hand on a table, again encouraging the children to copy you and join in.
3. Change the rhythm and move different parts of the body, with children copying and joining in.
4. Talk about the different rhythms you can make by stressing one syllable more than another and try some of them out together.

Think, do, review

Think – Think about how both speed and rhythm might affect body movements. Try this out with some examples for the children to see this for themselves.

Do – In pairs, ask pupils to tap or clap repeated rhythms for each other to move to.

⇨ *SEN support: Use adult support to stimulate ideas.*

⇨ *Extension: Ask able pupils to compose and practise a series of repeated rhythms and movements.*

Review – Ask each pair to join with another pair, showing each other what they did and discussing how well rhythms and movements went together.

Thinking skills

Enqu	
Prob	
Crea	●
Info	
Reas	
Eval	

Transfer and compare

● As a class, listen to a repeated rhythm. Now encourage the children to think of some words to fit the rhythm and chant these together. Repeat the exercise with children working in pairs or small groups, making up their own rhythms and chants.

⇨ *SEN support: Use adult support to stimulate ideas.*

⇨ *Extension: Ask able pupils to compose a rap.*

● Listen to some of the chants and raps. Compare this task of fitting words to a rhythm with the previous task of putting rhythm and movements together.

Thinking about thinking

Help pupils to assess the thinking skills they have used in this activity and, if time allows, record them in their Thinking Books.

Think-links

Help the children think of situations in other subjects where creative thinking skills using a repeated pattern can be used, such as:

Literacy – compose songs, jingles and raps;

ICT – create puzzles and problems using shape patterns and sequences;

Art and design – design wrapping paper using repeating patterns;

PE – create movement sequences linked to specific musical themes.

The Romans are Coming!

Roman soldiers were marching across some fields when they came to a river. On the other side they could see a village of thatched huts. Beyond the village there was a forest.

The Romans could see a wooden fence all around the village. In the village, some women were grinding corn and weaving cloth, with children feeding chickens and playing nearby. In the fields outside the fence, men were looking after their animals and gathering in the harvest.

One of the men saw Romans coming and shouted out. All the villagers stopped what they were doing and ran to the main gate.

With a partner, discuss and decide:

- What did the Roman soldiers think when they saw the village?
- What did the villagers think when they saw the Romans marching towards them?
- How can the Romans cross the river? *(If you have time you could design something to help them get across.)*
- What should the villagers do? *(Make a plan for the villagers.)*

Thinking skills

Enqu	
Prob	
Crea	●
Info	●
Reas	●
Eval	

The Romans are Coming!

(Note: An alternative version of this activity would be to replace the Romans approaching a village with Vikings in longships approaching land.)

Main learning objective: to generate imaginative ideas and consider alternative points of view in a historical situation and to record information using a given format.

Connect and prepare

1. Elicit from pupils what they remember about the characteristics of Roman soldiers. (What did they look like? How did they travel? How did they behave?)

2. Now ask similar questions about the inhabitants of Britain before the Romans settled here. (Who were they? What were they like? How did they live?)

Think, do, review

Think – Ask pupils to think about what Roman soldiers might have been thinking about the Anglo-Saxons and vice versa. List the children's ideas on the board.

Do – Hand out copies of the activity sheet and, working in pairs, ask the pupils to read the short paragraph at the top of the sheet. Now go through the questions together, writing down key ideas to share later in the lesson.

⇨ **SEN support:** *Assist these pupils by scribing their ideas as a group.*

Review – As a class, share and discuss some of the answers. Now, with the children's contributions, begin drawing a class flow chart on the board showing what has happened so far. It should look something like this:

Roman soldiers march across the fields.

↓

They see a village.

↓

The villagers see the soldiers coming.

↓

Transfer and compare

● Ask the pupils to copy this first part of the flow chart at the top of a new page.

● Write the following question on the board, asking pupils not to say anything, but just to start thinking about what their answer might be:

 – What do you think will happen when the Romans get across the river?

- Ask the pupils, in their pairs, to discuss and decide what they think will happen, then fill in their sequence of actions to complete the flow chart.

  ⇨ *SEN support: an adult could scribe a group flow chart from their ideas.*

  ⇨ *Extension: Encourage able children to find out about any real situations (e.g. Roman attacks on villages) and compare them with what they thought might happen.*

- As a class, or with another pair, compare pupils' predictions and flow charts.

Thinking about thinking

Help pupils to assess the thinking skills they have used in this activity and, if time allows, record them in their Thinking Books.

Think-links

Encourage the children to identify other areas of the curriculum where they can use these information processing and reasoning skills, such as:

Science – record the stages and outcomes of investigations;

ICT – follow a simulation to model a sequence of actions;

PSHE – set a scene, predict what will happen and discuss outcomes/alternatives.

Christmas Crackers

Part A

- If just two people want to pull a cracker together, how many crackers do they need?
- If three people want to pull crackers with each other, how many crackers do they need?
- What about if a family of four people want to pull crackers with each other, how many crackers will they need?

Part B

Imagine a group of five people wanting to pull crackers with each other. How many crackers do you think they will need?

- First make an estimate and write it down.
- Then see if you can work it out and write down the answer.
- Did your answer come close to your estimate?

Part C

This time, you have to buy enough crackers for six people to be able to pull crackers with each other.

- How can you work out the answer?
- Do any of your previous answers give you any clues?
- Make an estimate first and write this down.
- Then try it out and see what answer you come to.
- Compare your answer with your estimate.
- Now compare with others in your group.
- If you have time, discuss how many crackers you might need for seven people, or more.

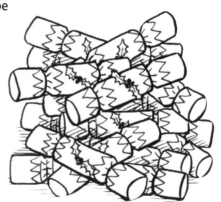

Christmas Crackers

Curriculum coverage

Ly	
Ny	●
Sc	>
ICT	
RE	
Hi	
Gg	>
DT	>
AD	
Mu	
PE	>
PSHE	

Thinking skills

Enqu	●
Prob	●
Crea	●
Info	
Reas	
Eval	

Main learning objective: to consider how to address a problem, plan possible strategies to use and try alternative approaches.

Connect and prepare

1. Ask the class to think about what people need to celebrate Christmas that they don't use at any other time of year. Record their ideas as a list on the board.

2. Set the scene: Many people like to get together with their families for Christmas. Everyone usually likes to pull a cracker with everyone else, and this is the problem we need to solve – how many crackers will we need if there are a lot of people there?

Think, do, review

Think – What do we need to know and how can we work out the answer? Write any ideas up on the board (e.g. How many people? Could we draw pictures or diagrams? Or use objects? Or act it out?).

Do – Distribute the activity sheet, read through Part A together and discuss how to find the answers for the examples given. Write the children's suggestions/answers on the board. Challenge pupils to try Part B together in pairs. (They can use any method they wish, but give them a time limit, to prevent them making designer crackers!)

⇨ *SEN support: Suggest SEN pupils use objects and work together as a group, with an adult's help.*

⇨ *Extension: Suggest able pupils they go on to Part C when they are ready.*

Review – Share and compare methods and answers. Ask some children to show others what they did and evaluate how successful their methods were.

Transfer and compare

● Using all that they have learnt so far, ask the children, working in pairs, to look at Part C of the activity sheet and discuss what method to use to try to work out the answers for larger numbers of people. Allow them time to see if they can work out the answers.

⇨ *SEN support: Take SEN pupils through each step, using a multi-sensory approach, with an adult keeping a careful note of how many, etc.*

⇨ *Extension: Ask able pupils if they notice any patterns in the answers so far that they could use to predict how many crackers would be needed for much larger numbers of people. How could they record this?*

- As a class, share and compare methods and answers. Ask able pupils to explain their ideas and findings.

Thinking about thinking

Help pupils to assess the thinking skills they have used in this activity and, if time allows, record them in their Thinking Books.

Think-links

Encourage children to think of other curriculum areas where they can use enquiry, problem solving and creative thinking skills to tackle a problem, such as:

Science – investigations, using findings to help predict further outcomes;

Geography – design a new housing estate taking amenities and access into consideration;

PE – children to work out a way of completing the given activities in the least time (safely!).

CHAPTER 4

Activities – Term 2

This chapter includes lesson plans and activity sheets for the following *Think About It!* activities.

Snakes and Lizards

A logic-tree

You can use the logic-tree below to find out whether you have found a snake or a lizard.

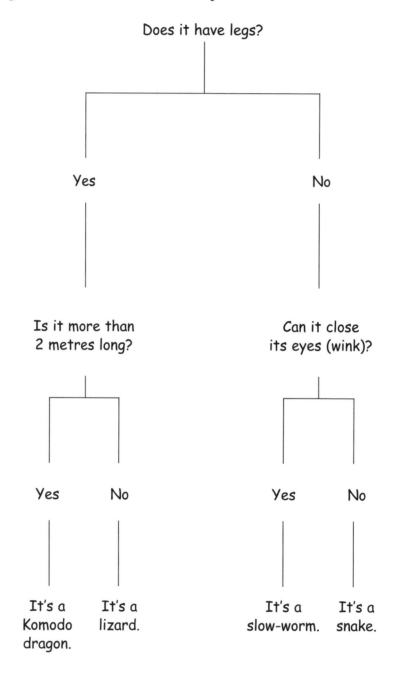

Does it have legs?

Yes — No

Yes: Is it more than 2 metres long?

Yes — It's a Komodo dragon.

No — It's a lizard.

No: Can it close its eyes (wink)?

Yes — It's a slow-worm.

No — It's a snake.

Snakes and Lizards

Main learning objective: Use a logic-tree to collect and classify information

Connect and prepare

1. Provide access to information books about different kinds of animals, different materials, or anything else that can be classified.
2. With the class discuss differences between groups of animals (e.g. mammals) and between animals within groups (e.g. big cats).
3. Hand out copies of the activity sheet and introduce pupils to the idea of classification by showing them the snakes and lizards logic-tree. Go through it together and discuss how it works.

Think, do, review

Think – Ask the children what kinds of questions would work in a logic-tree and what wouldn't. (Help them to see that questions need to have clear 'yes' or 'no' answers – probe this further by asking why not 'maybe' or 'sometimes'?).

Do – Ask for a confident child volunteer to come out to the front of the class. Write up on the board: 'Is it a human or an ape?'. Ask pupils to think of some questions to help them decide. (Give them thinking time first.) Draw and fill in the logic-tree on the board. It might look something like this:

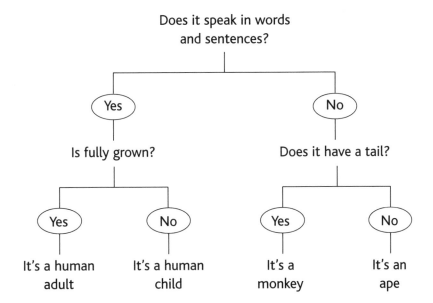

Is it an ape or a human?

Questions might include: 'Does it speak in words and sentences?', then 'Is it fully grown?' on the 'yes' side, and 'Does it have a tail?' on the 'no' side. The bottom line could read 'It's a human adult/child.' For the 'yes'/'no', respectively, on the left-hand side of the tree, 'It's a monkey/ape. For the 'yes'/'no', respectively, on the right-hand side of the tree (apes don't have tails).

Curriculum coverage

Ly	○>
Ny	
Sc	●
ICT	
RE	>
Hi	
Gg	>
DT	
AD	>
Mu	
PE	>
PSHE	

Thinking skills

Enqu	●
Prob	
Crea	
Info	●
Reas	
Eval	

Review – Once complete, follow this logic-tree through together for the child volunteer. Are pupils happy with the way it works, or would changes improve it?

Transfer and compare

- Ask pupils, working in pairs, to use information books (or the Internet) and choose another subject to classify (e.g. animals such as big cats, farmyard animals, pets, insects, etc., or types of materials, vehicles, dinosaurs). They should work together to design a logic-tree for their chosen subject and try it out to make sure it works.

  ⇨ *SEN support: Provide SEN pupils with specific questions and the books/information they will need. Alternatively have an adult work through the activity with them.*

  ⇨ *Extension: Encourage able pupils to build more options/branches and outcomes into their logic-trees.*

- Share outcomes in groups or as a whole class and discuss how well these outcomes worked.

Thinking about thinking

Help pupils to assess the thinking skills they have used in this task and, if time allows, record them in their Thinking Books.

Think-links

Encourage pupils to use logic-trees in other subjects, to differentiate or classify:

Literacy – story characters' attributes in order to tell which stories/genres they belong to;

RE – aspects of different rites or celebrations;

Geography – features of locations to find out where they are;

Art and design – differences between artists' styles; to tell who a painting is by;

PE – rules and features of different sports; which games are they?

Lost!

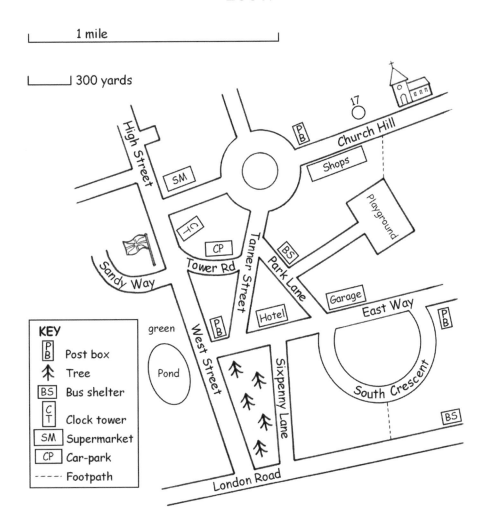

Part A

- You are going to a friend's house for his party.
- You've never been there before and now you are lost!
- Your friend lives at 17 Church Hill.
- You don't know exactly where you are, but you are standing on some grass.
- On your right you can see a duck pond.
- On your left, across a road, you can see a flag pole with a flag flying.
- In front of you there is a post box.
- Mark a cross on your map where you are standing.

Part B

- Can you see Church Hill on the map?
- Now see if you can find the best way to walk there.
- Mark your route on the map.
- Now work out the directions and write them down, saying what things you pass on the way.

© Jacquie Buttriss and Ann Callander (2005) *Think About It!*, David Fulton Publishers Ltd.

Ly	>
Ny	
Sc	
ICT	
RE	
Hi	
Gg	●
DT	
AD	
Mu	
PE	>
PSHE	

Thinking skills

Enqu	
Prob	●
Crea	
Info	
Reas	●
Eval	●

Lost!

Main learning objective: To use a map to consider a range of possible solutions to a problem, try them out and review how effective they were.

Connect and prepare

1. Show the class some maps and introduce the children to the idea of using a map to find your way.

2. On the board draw a simple map of the school in its area and ask the class to help you draw in landmarks. Discuss how to draw things simply.

3. Ask the children if they know what a 'key' is on a map. Make a simple 'key' together for your map on the board. Discuss how to use it and the landmarks to tell someone the way.

Think, do, review

Think – Give out copies of the 'Lost!' activity sheet and ask the class to look at the map. Explain to the children that they are lost on their way to a party and need to use the map to find their way. Read through Part A of the instructions together and ask if anyone can work out where they are. When they think they know, they should discuss it with a partner, agree and mark a cross where they think they are on the map.

Do – Challenge pupils to read the instructions in Part B and, working in pairs, to work out the best route, trying out different suggestions until they decide on the shortest or best route and mark it on their maps. Then ask them to work out and write down the directions for their best route. Could they use landmarks shown in the key to help them?

⇨ **SEN support:** *Guide SEN pupils through the task or give them clues.*

⇨ **Extension:** *Ask able pupils to use the distance guide to give more detailed directions.*

Review – As a class, share the different routes chosen and ask the children to give reasons for their choices. A volunteer could read out his or her directions for the rest of the class to follow on their maps. Discuss how clear and direct these directions were.

Transfer and compare

Now give the children two different locations on the map and ask them to find their way between them (e.g. from the bus shelter on London Road to the supermarket). Ask the pupils to write down a new set of directions between these two locations, then working in small groups get them to try out each others' routes to see how well they work.

⇨ *SEN support: For SEN pupils give fairly short, easy routes that require only brief directions to be written down.*

⇨ *Extension: Ask able pupils to draw maps of the area where they live, showing the main features and landmarks, and writing out directions for a walk around the neighbourhood.*

Thinking about thinking

Help pupils to assess the thinking skills they have used in this activity and, if time allows, record them in their Thinking Books.

Think-links

Challenge pupils to think of ways they could use maps or plans in other subjects, such as:

Literacy – work out a map to accompany a story, such as Red Riding Hood's way to her grandma's house;

PE – ask children to devise plans of how to set out apparatus in the hall or how to plan an obstacle course for sports day.

Noah's Ark

The lions went in first.

The bears were behind the zebras.

The cows were in front of the horses.

The elephants went in third.

The sheep were behind the pigs.

The tigers were behind the lions.

The sheep were in front of the cows.

The monkeys were in front of the zebras.

The pigs were in between the bears and the sheep.

The monkeys followed the elephants.

Noah's Ark

Where do they live?

Kate lives in the second house in the street.

Noah's Ark

Who's who?

This Henry had six wives and was the last King Henry. He died in AD 1547.

This Henry married a French princess. He reigned for nine years at the beginning of the fifteenth century.

This Henry was murdered in the Tower of London in AD 1461.

This Henry was the son of William the Conqueror. He reigned from AD 1100–1135.

This Henry reigned for 14 years and died at the beginning of the sixteenth century. He was the father of the last King Henry.

This Henry became king when he was only nine-years-old. He reigned for 56 years and died in AD 1272.

 This Henry ruled most of France as well as England. He reigned from AD 1154–1189.

This Henry's reign started in the fourteenth century and ended in the fifteenth century.

Noah's Ark

Curriculum coverage

Ly	○
Ny	○
Sc	
ICT	
RE	●
Hi	●
Gg	
DT	
AD	>
Mu	>
PE	
PSHE	

Thinking skills

Enqu	
Prob	●
Crea	
Info	●
Reas	
Eval	

Main learning objectives: use the language of sequence, recognise time sequences, reorganise information sequentially and plan strategies to use to solve a problem.

Connect and prepare

1. Ask the children to share what they know about the story of Noah's Ark.
2. Read 'Noah's Ark' on activity sheet A and explain that the order in which the animals went into the ark has been muddled.
3. Ask the children to think of other activities where they have needed to arrange things in the correct order.

Think, do, review

Think – Challenge the children to think of ways of sorting out the order of the animals and explain that they can use anything in the classroom to help them, but they must be able to show the solution clearly to others in the class.

Do – In pairs or small groups, give the children a copy of activity sheet A and ask them to work through the clues together to solve the problem.

⇨ *SEN support: Give adult support for reading and provide visual/concrete materials to help with sequencing.*

⇨ *Extension: Challenge able children to make up a problem of their own, using either activity sheet B 'Where do they live?' as a starting point, or devising their own.*

Review – Ask the whole class to compare their ideas with others and review alternative solutions.

Transfer and compare

- As a class, talk about what is meant by the term 'chronological order'. Then decide on the strategies that could be used to complete the task on activity sheet C – 'Who's who?'. (Ensure that the children are aware that the fifteenth century actually means 1400–1500.)
- After completing the task together, compare the skills and strategies used with those used for 'Noah's Ark'.

Thinking about thinking

Help pupils to assess the thinking skills they have used in this activity and, if time allows, record them in their Thinking Books.

Think-links

Encourage the children to transfer the thinking skills they have used in this activity to other curriculum areas, such as:

Literacy – sequence events in a story, or sequencing instructions;

Numeracy – identify number sequences and patterns;

History – compile timelines;

Music – order rhythm and notation sequences in compositions;

Art and design – use pattern sequences in designs.

Once Upon a Time

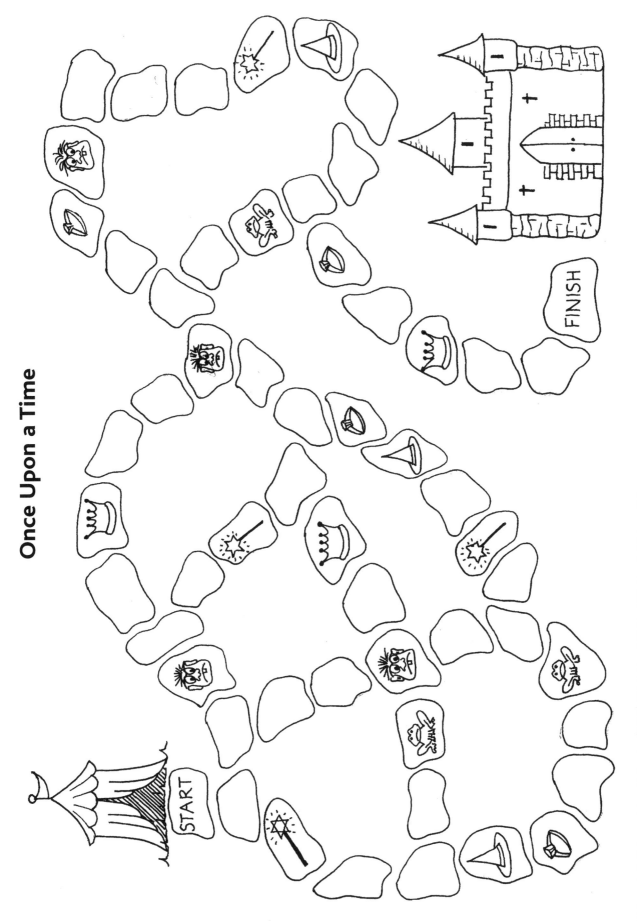

Once Upon a Time

Curriculum coverage

Ly	●
Ny	●
Sc	
ICT	>
RE	
Hi	
Gg	
DT	>
AD	
Mu	
PE	>
PSHE	

Main learning objectives: to generate imaginative ideas; record information using own format; recognise similarities and differences in outcomes.

Connect and prepare

1. Show the children a Snakes and Ladders baseboard and ask them to talk about how the game is played. Do all board games need rules? Ask the children to give reasons for their answers.

2. If we changed the rules for Snakes and Ladders, how would it alter the game? Ask the children to suggest some ideas.

Think, do, review

Thinking skills

Enqu	
Prob	
Crea	●
Info	●
Reas	
Eval	

Think – Show the class two baseboards, one with pictures and symbols (see the activity sheet entitled 'Once Upon a Time') and one without (see the second activity sheet). Ask the pupils to think of ideas for a game using one of these baseboards.
Do – Give the children the choice of working individually or with a partner to create a new game. Remind them that they will need to write clear instructions for playing the game and, in the case of the blank baseboard, they will need to think of some rewards and hazards.

⇨ *SEN support: Allow the children to record their instructions on an audio tape or use a scribe.*

⇨ *Extension: Challenge able pupils to design their own baseboard using a different layout, or to devise a game with both simple and more complex rules.*

Review – Ask the children to trial their games and discuss possible improvements.

Transfer and compare

Give the children some time to make any improvements to their games. Then, in groups, ask them to compare their games with others and discuss similarities and differences.

Thinking about thinking

Help pupils to assess the thinking skills they have used in this activity and, if time allows, record them in their Thinking Books.

Think-links

Encourage the children to transfer the thinking skills they have used in this activity to other curriculum areas, such as:

ICT – combine text and graphics to develop games, mazes and puzzles;

DT – develop games and mazes, using both 2D and 3D materials;

PE – devise own rules and instructions for games, using specific equipment.

Plague Village

In the year 1665, there was a great plague which spread across the whole of Britain. A parcel of cloth was sent to a man who lived in the village of Eyam. He was a tailor. The man opened up his parcel and took out the cloth to have a good look at it. While he was deciding what to make with his cloth, he did not see

the fleas that were hiding in the cloth. They jumped out and bit the man.

A few days later, the tailor became very ill. His neighbours looked after him. Later that week the tailor died. Then his neighbours became ill and they also died. Soon other neighbours became ill and died. This was a very serious illness called the plague. Before long, there were people in several houses in the village who had become ill with the plague. It spread all over the village of Eyam.

The people who lived in other villages in the area became very frightened when they saw what was happening.

The people who lived in Eyam talked about it and made a very brave decision. They closed the village off. Nobody could come into the village and nobody could leave it. This went on for more than a year.

Plague Village

Ly	○
Ny	
Sc	
ICT	○
RE	>
Hi	●
Gg	>
DT	
AD	
Mu	
PE	
PSHE	

Main learning objective: To ask questions to explore reasons for events and think creatively about how to solve related problems.

Connect and prepare

Ask the children about how people get illnesses and introduce the idea of 'catching' diseases – how is this most likely to happen; how can it be prevented, or cured? Have any of them caught illnesses from other people? Introduce the term 'infectious' diseases. Brainstorm a list of infectious diseases. If the plague hasn't been included, introduce it. Explain how serious this used to be and why it couldn't be cured (before antibiotics were invented).

Thinking skills

Enqu	●
Prob	
Crea	●
Info	
Reas	
Eval	

Think, do, review

Think – With the class read the account of Plague Village provided on the activity sheet. Ask the children to reread it for themselves and take time to think about the questions:
– Why did the people of Eyam close their village?
– Why was it a brave decision?
Ask the pupils to share and compare their ideas about this, then consider and discuss:
– Do you think everyone was happy about this (a) in the village? or b) in the surrounding area?
Do – Now ask the children, working in pairs, to think about the problems that might arise when the village was closed for a long time. Make a list of the things the people of the village might have needed to plan for (e.g. food, water, health and medicines, work, education, family, news, rubbish disposal).

⇨ *SEN support: An adult to guide and prompt, or provide a 'crib-sheet' of questions.*

⇨ *Extension: Challenge able pupils to draw up a detailed plan to address the villagers' needs.*

Review – Discuss and list on the board the issues that would need to be planned for.

Transfer and compare

● Ask the children, working in pairs, to go through the list of issues and discuss how they would deal with each issue in turn. They must decide what the best solutions would be, making notes to help them remember.

⇨ *Extension: Encourage able children to find out (using books or the Internet) what actually happened and how the people of Eyam addressed these problems for themselves.*

- Now, as a class, share the solutions and reasoning. Evaluate their potential effectiveness.

- Ask the able researchers to feed back their findings to the class, or tell the children yourself what actually happened and what solutions the people of Eyam adopted to address their problems. What arrangements surprised pupils the most and why?

Thinking about thinking

Help pupils to assess the thinking skills they have used in this activity and, if time allows, record them in their Thinking Books.

Think-links

Encourage the children to identify other subject areas where enquiry skills and creative thinking skills could be used to solve problems. For example in:

Literacy – read the first part of a story in which a problematical situation arises, then stop to ask the children to plan ahead and predict a range of possible outcomes;

RE – situations described in the Bible, such as the story of Joseph in Egypt;

Geography – discuss the situations which can occur in severe weather conditions or natural disasters, such as hurricanes, floods, landslides or earthquakes.

Something to Drink

Storyteller:	It was a hot day. A crow and his friends were looking for something to drink.
Crow:	Look! Here's an old jug.
Blackbird:	Is there any water in it?
Starling:	Let's have a look inside.
Storyteller:	They landed and looked in the jug.
Crow:	I can just see some water at the bottom.
Blackbird:	We can't reach it.
Starling:	The neck of the jug is too narrow.
Crow:	So how can we get the water out?
Storyteller:	The birds sat and thought about the problem.
Blackbird:	Why don't we tip the jug on its side?
Starling:	Then the water will run out and we can all have a drink.
Storyteller:	The crow looked at the jug.
Crow:	But if we tip the water out, it will soak into the ground.
Blackbird:	Oh dear! That's not a good idea.
Starling:	We must think of something else.
Storyteller:	The crow put his head on one side and looked at the starling.
Crow:	Can you think of an idea?
Starling:	There are some small stones near the jug.
Crow:	Yes. We could make a pond with them.
Blackbird:	If we tip the jug over, the water will stay in the pond and we can all have a drink.
Storyteller:	The crow thought for a moment.
Crow:	But how will we move the stones?
Starling:	We can pick them up in our beaks.
Blackbird:	That's a good idea.
Storyteller:	The crow looked at the stones.
Crow:	But the stones are round. When we put them together there will be gaps between them.
Blackbird:	And the water will run away between the gaps.
Starling:	Oh dear. I never thought of that.
Storyteller:	By now, all the birds were feeling very thirsty.
Crow:	We must find a way to get the water, somehow.
Blackbird:	I'm sure we could do something with the stones.
Starling:	Yes, but what?
Crow:	I know!
Storyteller:	The blackbird and the starling looked at the crow.
Blackbird:	What can we do?
Starling:	Hurry up and tell us, I'm thirsty.
Crow:	I have a really great idea!
Blackbird:	But will it work?
Crow:	I think so.
Starling:	What is it?
Crow:	I'll show you.
Storyteller:	What do you think the Crow's idea was? Do you think it worked? Can you try out some ideas and help the birds solve the problem?

Thinking skills

Enqu	
Prob	●
Crea	
Info	
Reas	
Eval	●

Something to Drink

Main learning objectives: to recognise and talk about a problem; consider possible solutions; use senses to investigate materials; decide on criteria to evaluate quality of materials.

Connect and prepare

1. Explain to the children that this play has been adapted from one of *Aesop's Fables* ('The Crow and the Pitcher'). Ask the children to talk about fables they know.

2. Remind children that they will need to think carefully about what they read in this activity. They will need to use evidence in the text to help them solve the problem. They will also need to decide on ways of presenting their solutions to the class.

Think, do, review

Hand out copies of the activity sheet.

Think – Ask the children to read the play in groups of four (each taking one part). Then ask them to think about the birds' problem and discuss possible solutions.

⇨ *SEN support: Ensure that less able readers are in groups with more able readers. Prompt the children with open-ended questioning to give them opportunities to offer ideas.*

⇨ *Extension: Challenge able children to consider the same situation but where the birds found the jug on a sandy beach. How do you think they would have solved the problem?*

Do – Ask the groups to prepare and then present their solutions to the class.
Review – Ask the children, as a class or in pairs/groups, to consider:
– How practical were the solutions?
– How clearly presented were they?

Transfer and compare

Show the class a range of materials the birds have found to build their nests. Allow children to handle the materials and then ask them to decide on a criterion for judging the most suitable materials for nest building.

Thinking about thinking

Help pupils to assess the thinking skills they have used in this activity and, if time allows, record them in their Thinking Books.

Think-links

Encourage the children to transfer the thinking skills they have used in this activity to other problem-solving activities. These could include:

Numeracy – solve problems using shapes, patterns and reflective symmetry;

Science – investigate possible solutions to problems such as moving objects from one place to another, only using certain materials;

DT – design and construct models only using certain materials;

PE – use suitable apparatus to help solve a specific problem, such as moving an object from one part of the room to another.

Ly	○
Ny	
Sc	>
ICT	●
RE	
Hi	>
Gg	●
DT	
AD	>
Mu	
PE	
PSHE	>

Thinking skills

Enqu	
Prob	
Crea	●
Info	
Reas	
Eval	

What If?

Main learning objectives: look at a familiar activity from a different viewpoint and use imagination to devise alternative activities.

Connect and prepare

1. Ask the children to identify their favourite TV programmes. Write five of the most popular programmes on the board and discuss reasons for their popularity.

2. Discuss together how much television is watched by the children in the class and how important they feel it is in their lives.

Think, do, review

Think – Ask the children: 'What if television had not been invented (including videos and DVDs), what would you do instead of watching television?' Urge the children to use their imagination to think of interesting ideas for activities.

Do – Encourage pupils to talk about their ideas in pairs and devise a mime to show these ideas to their class-mates.

⇨ *SEN support: Ask SEN pupils open-ended questions to elicit a discussion about their favourite activities, apart from watching television.*

⇨ *Extension: Challenge able pupils to devise a way of showing the amount of TV watched during a day and a detailed breakdown of how that could be replaced.*

Review – Each pair is to mime their ideas to another pair or to the group. Follow this with a class review of pupils' ideas for interest and enjoyment.

Transfer and compare

● Ask the children to consider how their daily lives might change if, in addition to no televisions, there were also no computers, CD players or mobile phones.

● Compare the implications of being without most of our modern technology rather than just being without television.

Thinking about thinking

Help pupils to assess the thinking skills they have used in this activity and, if time allows, record them in their Thinking Books.

Think-links

Encourage the children to transfer the thinking skills they have used in this activity to other curriculum areas. These could include:

Science – suggest creative ideas to solve scientific problems, such as how to make minibeast habitats in the school grounds;

History – develop empathy skills through role-play activities in order to imagine life in the past;

Art and design – design games to help children to practise a specific skill;

PSHE – find creative solutions to everyday social problems.

Making Music

(Note: This activity could be spread across two lessons.)

Main learning objective: Consider a range of possible solutions and their effects and generate imaginative ideas for controlling them.

Connect and prepare

1. Introduce the children to the idea of writing music down by asking them: 'In an orchestra, how do the musicians know how and when to play their instruments?'

2. Tell the class how the 'score' gives instructions for the whole orchestra so that they know what notes to play, how loudly, when and how long for.

Think, do, review

Think – Ask the children to think about different types of musical instruments, how they are played and what kind of sound each one produces. Do their sounds have anything to do with what they are made from? (List the main groups of instruments on the board.)

Do – Show the class the range of materials set out for them to use. Challenge the children to make their own instruments out of these materials (paper, straws, string, rice, peas, fabric, yoghurt pots, card, wood and anything else available).

Review – The children should evaluate their finished instruments by describing how it was made, how it is played and what kind of sound it produces. Is there any way to control or vary the sound (or can they think of a way of doing this)?

Transfer and compare

- Working in small groups challenge the pupils to make up some music to play with their instruments. Ensure that each group has a range of instrument types. The task is to compose a piece of music together and find a way of writing this down so that they will be able to practise it together to perform another day. The children need to think about how they can show what each instrument is doing and when, and how long for each note or beat. (Suggest they devise symbols.)

  ⇨ *SEN support: Provide adult help for SEN pupils to decide on and scribe the symbols for the group.*

  ⇨ *Extension: Ensure that able children use symbols that show when and how often to play each instrument, how long each note/beat should last and how loud it should be played.*

Curriculum coverage

Ly	>
Ny	
Sc	
ICT	
RE	
Hi	
Gg	
DT	●
AD	>
Mu	●
PE	>
PSHE	

Thinking skills

Enqu	
Prob	●
Crea	●
Info	
Reas	
Eval	●

Each group should write at least four bars of music, practise it together and play it to the class. Together evaluate the pieces of music and how well they have worked.

● If there is time, an additional evaluation task could be to be music reviewers and write a sentence about their or another group's performance.

Thinking about thinking

Help pupils to assess the thinking skills they have used in this activity and, if time allows, record them in their Thinking Books.

Think-links

Encourage the children to identify other subject areas where they can use the thinking skills used in this activity. For example:

Literacy/drama – introduce the use of story-boards to devise and perform role-play situations or short plays.

Art and design – choose and control a range of art techniques to produce a particular effect.

PE – select a range of moves or actions and then using these devise, practise and perform a sequence of movements.

Toys and Games

Snakes and Ladders
The oldest known board is wooden. It was made in 1640.

Kite
People think that the kite was invented by General Han Sin in China during the second century BC.

Dominoes
Objects made of bone that looked similar to dominoes were found in Iraq. They were dated around 2450 BC. The game of dominoes was first played in Britain at the end of the eighteenth century.

Chess
People think that this game was first played in India in the sixth century. The rules that we use today were first used in 1550.

Marbles
There is evidence to show that different forms of this game have been played since human beings were on Earth.

Computer games
The first computer games were invented in the 1980s.

Video games
The first video game was invented in 1972.

Lego
The first Lego bricks were sold in 1955.

Scrabble
Scrabble was invented by a man called Alfred M. Butts in 1931. It was patented and sold by a man called James Brunot in 1948.

Model cars
The first model cars were made at the end of the nineteenth century.

Jigsaw puzzles
Jigsaw puzzles were first sold around 1760. At this time they were often pictures of maps and were used as educational toys.

Teddy bears
The first teddy bears were being sold in about 1902.

© Jacquie Buttriss and Ann Callander (2005) *Think About It!*, David Fulton Publishers Ltd.

Thinking skills

Enqu	
Prob	
Crea	
Info	●
Reas	
Eval	

Toys and Games

Main learning objective: to talk about and recognise time sequences and sort information using a given structure.

Connect and prepare

1. Ask the children to share their prior understanding of key time concepts (century, BC, AD, and that the nineteenth century means 1800–1900) and ensure that they understand what is meant by a timeline.

2. Hand out copies of the activity sheet 'Toys and Games' and read it together.

Think, do, review

Think – Give the children a sheet of plain A4 paper and ask them to think about how they could make a timeline showing when each of the toys and games was first used.

Do – The children can work individually or in pairs to compile their timelines.

SEN support: Adult support will be needed for this activity as chronology is a complex concept and SEN children will need guidance.

Extension: Challenge able children to find out about when other toys and games, particularly unusual ones, were first used. Encourage them to use a range of information sources.

Review – Ask each pair to share and discuss their timeline with another pair.

Transfer and compare

As a class, look at some number pattern sequences which have numbers missing. Ask the children to suggest what the missing numbers should be, giving reasons for their choices. Compare the task of working with number pattern sequences with the previous task of making a timeline. How is it similar/different?

Thinking about thinking

Help pupils to assess the thinking skills they have used in this activity and, if time allows, record them in their Thinking Books.

Think-links

Encourage the children to transfer the thinking skills they have used in this activity to other areas of the curriculum. These could include:

Literacy – sequence events in a story or account, using the language of time;

Science – record experimental actions and their outcomes in the correct order;

History – organise people, events and other artefacts in chronological order;

RE – sequence major events from the Bible or from another religious source in chronological order.

Decisions and Consequences

Question	Yes	Consequence	No	Consequence
Your brother has a book that you need for homework but he is out. Do you borrow it without asking?				
You have broken one of your grandmother's china ornaments. Do you hide it and hope that she won't notice?				
You find a £1 coin in the playground. Do you take it straight to an adult?				
Your best friend has been horrid to you. Do you go and play with someone else?				
Your ball has gone over into your next door neighbour's garden. Do you go and get it without asking first?				

Decisions and Consequences

Question	Yes	Consequence	No	Consequence

Decisions and Consequences

Curriculum coverage

Ly	●
Ny	>
Sc	>
ICT	
RE	
Hi	>
Gg	●
DT	
AD	
Mu	
PE	
PSHE	●

Thinking skills

Enqu	
Prob	
Crea	
Info	
Reas	●
Eval	

Main learning objectives: to give reasons for ideas and actions and to understand the concept of cause and effect.

Connect and prepare

1. As a class, discuss the two words 'decision' and 'consequence'. Ask pupils to share some decisions that they have made and their consequences.

2. Hand out copies of 'Decisions and Consequences' activity sheet A and ask the children to consider the first scenario together and discuss it. Talk about both 'Yes' and 'No' answers and their consequences.

Think, do, review

Think – Give the children time to read the other scenarios on activity sheet A and consider the situations.

Do – Ask the children, working in pairs, to discuss each of the situations in turn and to complete their answers, together or separately, on the sheet, giving clear reasons for their opinions.

⇨ *SEN support: Provide reading support as well as some open-ended questions to encourage the children to think through their ideas.*

⇨ *Extension: Challenge able children to devise their own scenarios on activity sheet B, then swap with a partner to predict the consequences.*

Review – Ask the children, as a class or in pairs/groups, to consider:
– Have you explained the consequences clearly?
– Could other children's ideas change your decisions?

Transfer and compare

● Set the class the following challenge – Suppose that it has been decided that a new classroom should be built on part of the playground. As governors of the school, you and your partner have to decide whether you agree with the proposals or not and what the consequences of your decision might be.

● As a class, consider how this discussion differs from those on Activity Sheet A (e.g. does this situation have wider implications?)

Thinking about thinking

Help pupils to assess the thinking skills they have used in this activity and, if time allows, record them in their Thinking Books.

Think-links

Encourage the children to transfer the thinking skills they have used in this activity to other areas of the curriculum, such as:

Literacy – Shared and Guided reading: express opinions on characters' actions and predicting consequences;

Numeracy – Predict the probability of yes and no answers for a number of situations, giving consequences for whichever is most likely;

Science – investigate the relationships between causes and effects of certain processes, such as heating or freezing, on a variety of materials;

History – investigate possible causes and effects of activities and events in the past;

Geography – identify extreme weather conditions, such as hurricanes, thunderstorms, floods, thick fog, blizzards, etc., and their effects on both people and the environment.

End Product

You can use these items in any way that you choose but you must use all of them.

one A4 sheet of white card

three coloured straws

two pieces of coloured wool (each 30 cm long)

scraps of coloured paper

scraps of coloured tissue paper

felt-tip pens

wax crayons

pencil

glue

scissors

ruler

Thinking skills

Enqu	
Prob	
Crea	●
Info	
Reas	
Eval	

End Product

Main learning objectives: to generate and extend ideas creatively, experiment with different materials and apply imaginative thinking.

Connect and prepare

1. Ask the children, as a class, to make connections between specific objects and suggested activities (e.g. cup/drinking, fork/eating, shoes/walking, pencil/writing, etc.).

2. Ask the pupils to think of different and unusual ways in which these everyday items could be used. Encourage creative thinking and list their ideas on the board.

Think, do, review

Think – Display the items listed on the activity sheet and hand out copies of the sheet so the children can read through the task. Give the children a few minutes individual thinking time. Remind them they can make whatever they like, but they must use *all* the items in some way during the process. Now allow them to discuss their ideas with a partner.

Do – Ask the children to decide whether to work alone or with a partner. They should first draw a design for an end product which will use all the items, then label it.

⇨ *SEN support: Encourage SEN children to try out their ideas using scrap paper and talk about this.*

⇨ *Extension: Challenge able pupils to write or draw their instructions, noting any design changes or improvements.*

Review – Ask pupils, as a class or in pairs/groups, to consider:
– How clear are their designs?
– What changes might be needed when actually making their end products?

Transfer and compare

● Ask the pupils to transfer their design ideas into making the end product. Encourage imaginative ideas through open-ended questioning of individuals/pairs.

● Ask the children to present their 'end products' to the class and compare them with their original designs.

Thinking about thinking

Help pupils to assess the thinking skills they have used in this activity and, if time allows, record them in their Thinking Books.

Think-links

Encourage the children to transfer their creative thinking skills to other areas of the curriculum, such as:

Science – create a game using magnets and a range of materials;

Music – create music out of a range of materials and objects in the classroom (e.g. paper, pencils, pots, jars, etc.);

Art and design – provide a variety of collage materials and ask pupils to consider what subject these would suit, what materials they will select and how they will use them;

PE – make up a gymnastic sequence, using specific apparatus.

Ly	●
Ny	
Sc	
ICT	
RE	
Hi	>
Gg	>
DT	
AD	
Mu	
PE	
PSHE	●

Thinking skills

Enqu	
Prob	●
Crea	
Info	
Reas	
Eval	●

Playground Problems

Main learning objectives: to identify causes of problems and their effects; to discuss problems and consider possible solutions; to evaluate the quality of solutions; to predict possible outcomes.

Connect and prepare

1. As a class ask the children to brainstorm some of the problems related to playtimes. Write their ideas on the board.

2. Ask the pupils to organise themselves into groups of four and choose one of the problems to discuss. (Ensure that each group chooses a different problem to discuss.)

Think, do, review

Think – One pupil writes down the problem on a piece of card for each group. Give the children individual quiet thinking time, before asking them to discuss possible solutions with their groups.

Do – The groups talk about possible solutions and decide on the most feasible.

⇨ **SEN support:** *To encourage SEN pupils use prompt and praise techniques during the group discussion.*

⇨ **Extension:** *Challenge able pupils to consider some of the reasons for the 'playground problems' and the consequences of alternative solutions.*

Review – One child from each group moves to another group to share problems and ideas for solutions. Review the children's ideas for their practicality.

Transfer and compare

- Ask each group to choose a spokesperson to present both the problem and the most practical solution to the class. Ask the group to consider: if only one problem and solution could be considered, then how could you persuade others to choose yours?

- The class votes for the solution children think would improve playtimes the most.

Thinking about thinking

Help pupils to assess the thinking skills they have used in this activity and, if time allows, record them in their Thinking Books.

Think-links

Encourage the children to transfer the thinking skills they have used in this activity to other areas of the curriculum, such as:

Literacy – identify cause and effect in stories and consider alternative outcomes.

History – identify causes and effects of events in history and consider what might have happened if alternative decisions had been made.

Geography – identify environmental problems and suggest possible solutions.

CHAPTER 5

Activities – Term 3

This chapter includes lesson plans and activity sheets for the following *Think About It!* activities.

Pirates!

Buried treasure

Pirate is the name given to anyone who tries to capture ships or steal from ships carrying people or cargo across the seas. Long ago, when pirates captured a ship, they stole anything that they thought they might need. This could include food, drink, clothes, medicines or weapons, as well as money, jewels and other valuable items. The money, jewels and valuables were often kept in a large chest by the pirate captain. This was the treasure chest. Some pirates hid these treasure chests on small islands. They drew maps and wrote clues to show where the treasure was hidden. Many pirates were caught and hanged before they could go back and find their treasure. So all over the world there are islands still hiding pirates' buried treasure.

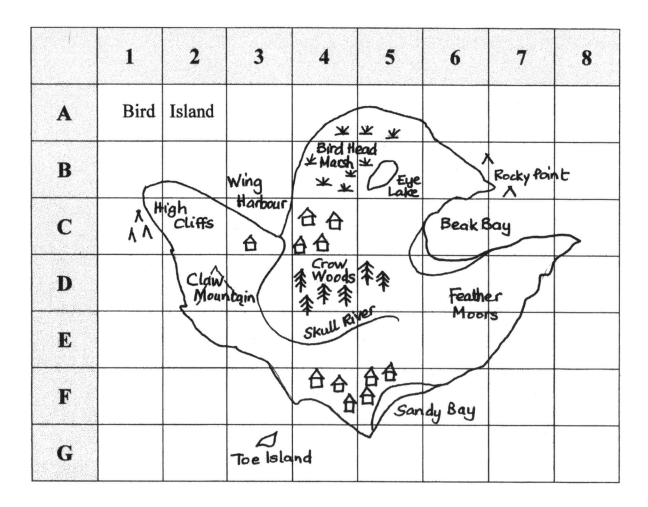

Pirates!

Treasure Island

The island is shaped like a boat. It has two bays, one on each side of the island. It has a river running from a mountain range in the centre of the island to one of the bays. A thick jungle is on one side of the island. On the other side are steep cliffs with rocky paths and hidden caves. Around one of the bays there are some old buildings that are no longer used. A small stream flows from the river into a lake at the foot of the mountain range.

	1	2	3	4	5	6	7	8
A								
B								
C								
D								
E								
F								
G								

Enqu	
Prob	
Crea	
Info	●
Reas	
Eval	

Pirates!

Main learning objectives: to use relevant information and present it in a given format; to talk about similarities and differences in formats.

Connect and prepare

1. Discuss what pupils know about pirates. Hand out copies of 'Pirates' activity sheet A. Read the information on 'Buried treasure'.

2. Ask the children to look carefully at the map of Bird Island, guess where the treasure might be buried and mark this square with a cross. Then give three clues as to where the treasure is buried (two relating to the location and the third being the grid reference, e.g. C4). How many children marked the correct square? Which was the easiest clue?

Think, do, review

Think – Ask the children to read the description of 'Treasure Island' with a partner and think about the best place on this island to hide treasure.
Do – Using the description, ask children to draw a treasure map on the blank grid and write co-ordinate clues for finding the treasure, starting where the pirates land.

⇨ *SEN support: Allow SEN children to record their clues using an audio tape, or use a scribe.*

⇨ *Extension: Challenge able children to compile a key for the treasure map and put additional features on the island.*

Review – Tell each pair to ask another pair to find their hidden treasure. They should then review the accuracy of their co-ordinates.

Transfer and compare

● Show a page in a big book atlas or a large map and ask pupils to locate places using the grid references.

● Compare this task with the treasure map task and discuss similarities and differences.

Thinking about thinking

Help pupils to assess the thinking skills they have used in this activity and, if time allows, record them in their Thinking Books.

Think-links

Encourage the children to transfer the thinking skills used in this activity to other areas of the curriculum, such as:

Geography – learn to use co-ordinates on road maps or Ordnance Survey maps;

English – write clues and instructions for a variety of purposes;

Science – use a letter/number co-ordinate grid to plot where minibeasts were found;

ICT – write instructions to direct a programmable robot or to draw shapes on the screen;

PE – write and/or use instructions for orienteering activities within the school environment.

Fossil Hunter

Mary Anning lived with her family at Lyme Regis, in Dorset. Mary's father had a small shop that sold sea shells and fossils. In those days only rich people could afford to have holidays by the sea, so they were the most likely people to buy things from the shop. Every day Mary and her father collected interesting sea shells along the seashore and fossils from the rocks. Mary's father showed her how to remove fossils without damaging them.

In 1810, when Mary was 11, her father died and Mary had to collect sea shells and fossils on her own. She needed to have enough to sell in the shop to support her mother and family.

One day Mary found a large pile of rocks that had fallen from the cliff. She saw some bones sticking out of the rock and began to use a small hammer to chip away at the rock. After a while she realised that the bones were part of a large skeleton and that she would need to ask for help. She thought that it might be the fossil of a monster animal that had lived many years ago.

Scientists were interested in the giant fossil and thought that it might have been a creature that lived both on land and in water. They called it ichthyosaurus (fish-lizard). It was 10 metres long and had a huge snout, like a beak, which was full of sharp teeth.

Mary also found the first fossil of a plesiosaur. Scientists thought that it might have been a sea creature. Some sailors said that they had seen creatures like it on their travels and called them sea-serpents, but no one could prove that these tales were true.

In 1828 Mary found the first fossil of a dimorphodon. Scientists thought that it might have been a flying reptile which looked like a huge bat. People from all over the world visited Lyme Regis so that they could meet Mary Anning and see where she had found the famous fossils. There is a stained-glass window, in a church in Lyme Regis, in memory of Mary. There is also a well-known tongue twister that people think refers to Mary. See if you can say it:

'She sells sea shells by the seashore.'

Fossil Hunter

Statement	Fact	Opinion
Mary Anning lived at Lyme Regis in Dorset.		
Mary had to earn enough money to support her mother and family when she was 11.		
Only rich people bought sea shells and fossils in the shop.		
Mary's father died in 1810.		
Mary knew how to remove fossils from rocks without damaging them.		
The large skeleton may have been a monster animal.		
The ichthyosaurus skeleton was 10 metres long.		
The fossil of the plesiosaur was the same creature that sailors said that they saw on their travels.		

Enqu	
Prob	
Crea	
Info	
Reas	●
Eval	

Fossil Hunter

Main learning objective: to discern between fact and opinion; recognise and challenge assumptions.

Connect and prepare

1. Ask the children to tell you what they know about fossils.

2. Tell them that scientists use different methods of deciding on the age of a fossil but they have to rely on clues and their own opinion about how these animals and plants lived. Some of what we know about fossils is fact and some is opinion.

Think, do, review

Hand out copies of Activity sheets A and B.

Think – Explain to the children that some things that we read are facts (like names and dates) and some information tells us what people think about a subject, that is their opinion. Ask the children to read the information about Mary Anning on activity sheet A and see if they can find two facts.

Do – Tell the children to work with a partner to complete the grid on activity sheet B.

⇨ *SEN support: Allow children to record responses using audio tape, or use a scribe.*

⇨ *Extension: Using the information on Mary Anning, ask able pupils to write some additional fact and opinion statements about her in the spaces lower down on the sheet, for others to complete later.*

Review – The children should discuss their answers with another pair and then in a group.

Transfer and compare

As a class, share the extension group's additional statements and compare them with the original statements. Discuss how difficult it was to discern between fact and opinion in the whole text. Encourage the children to consider whether we can believe everything we read.

Thinking about thinking

Help pupils to assess the thinking skills they have used in this activity and, if time allows, record them in their Thinking Books.

Think-links

Encourage the children to transfer the thinking skills they have used in this activity to other areas of the curriculum. These could include:

Literacy – discern between fact and opinion in reports of events;

Science – explore facts and opinions relating to the attributes of animals, plants or materials;

History – discern between fact and opinion when using historical evidence.

Geography – investigate facts/opinions related to locations or environmental issues, remembering not to be swayed by popular opinion;

RE – discern between fact and opinion regarding aspects of different religions;

Art and design – look at paintings to see how much is realistic and how much is the artist's interpretation.

Roman Numbers

Many of the ancient number systems had different symbols for units, tens, hundreds and thousands. The Romans used:

I – 1
V – 5
X – 10
L – 50
C – 100
D – 500
M – 1000

(a) Can you write numbers 1 to 20 in Roman numerals?

(b) Can you write the number 21?

(c) What number is LXXXVI?

(d) How do you think the number 40 was written?

(e) If CM is 900, what number do you think MCM is?

(f) If you look at old books you may find the date of publication printed in Roman numerals.

MCMXXXVII is 1937 (1900 and 37).

If the date on a book is MCMLXXXVIII, when was it published?

(g) At the end of television programmes you will see the date when they were first produced. If a programme was first produced in MCMLCIX what year was it?

(h) Can you add 54 to CM and write it in Roman numerals?

(i) Now make up some addition sums using Roman numerals.

Roman Numbers

Ly	>
Ny	●
Sc	
ICT	
RE	>
Hi	●
Gg	
DT	
AD	
Mu	>
PE	
PSHE	

Main learning objectives: to investigate connections and relationships in numbers, use creative thinking to develop a new number system and record, using own format.

Connect and prepare

1. Ask the children to look at a hundred number square and talk about the way the numbers are arranged. Talk about the pattern of our number system.

2. Explain that when number systems were first used they were not all the same. Write out the Roman numerals for 1 to 10 on the board and encourage the children to talk about why they think they were written in this way.

Think, do, review

Think – Tell the class that the Roman numeral for 4 was IV, and that for 9 it was IX. Encourage them to think about and discuss possible reasons why the letters were written in that order (i.e. encourage them to see that 'I' before 'V' represents 1 less than 5).

Do – Ask the children, working in pairs, to answer as many questions as they can on the 'Roman Numbers' activity sheet.

⇨ *SEN support: Adapt the questions to suit the ability of the children but make sure that at least one question extends their thinking.*

⇨ *Extension: The Romans had no symbol for zero. Challenge able pupils to investigate how this might have affected them when they were doing mathematical calculations.*

Review – Encourage pupils to discuss their findings with another pair.

Thinking skills

Enqu	
Prob	
Crea	●
Info	●
Reas	
Eval	

Transfer and compare

- Ask the children to make up a number system (1 to 10) of their own using shapes or symbols. Discuss possible problems and solutions.

- Ask the children to consider how well their number system would work compared to that used by the Romans.

Thinking about thinking

Help pupils to assess the thinking skills they have used in this activity and, if time allows, record them in their Thinking Books.

Think-links

Encourage the children to transfer the thinking skills they have used in this activity to other areas of the curriculum, such as:

Literacy – create codes, riddles and anagrams;

Numeracy – investigate other number systems;

RE – investigate the use of signs and symbols in the environment, in our culture and in religions and what meanings they have;

Music – investigate the standard system of musical notation (different symbols representing notes of different durations, etc.)

Eating Habits

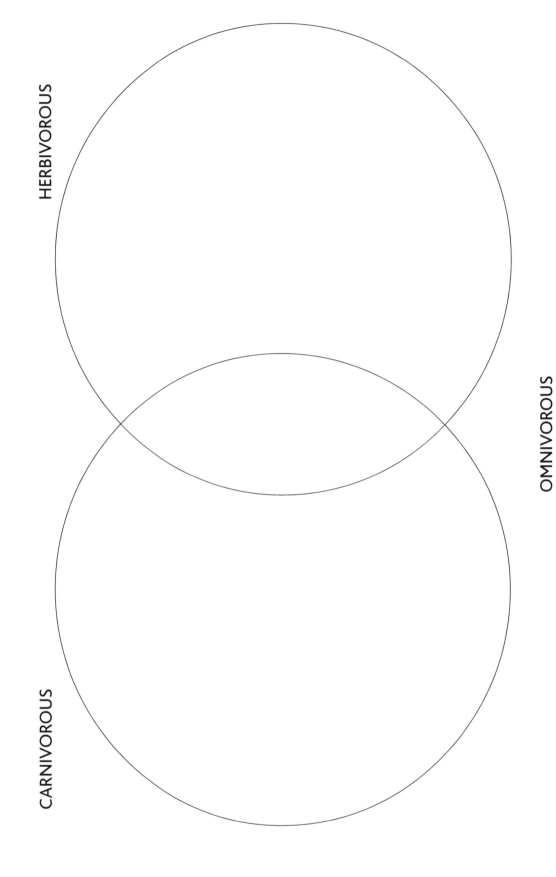

HERBIVOROUS

OMNIVOROUS

CARNIVOROUS

Eating Habits

Main learning objectives: know where to find information; use skimming and scanning strategies; collect and organise information using a given criteria; record using a given format.

Connect and prepare

1. Ask the children to share what they know about the words 'carnivorous', 'herbivorous' and 'omnivorous'.

2. Show the children a simple Venn diagram. Talk about how it works and the information we can learn from it.

Think, do, review

Think – Ask the children, working individually, to think of three animals: one that is carnivorous, one herbivorous and one omnivorous.

Do – With a partner, ask the children to use information material (books and the Internet) to check the eating habits of the three chosen animals. Hand at copies of the activity sheet and ask the pupils to write the animals in the correct place on the Venn diagram. Then using the information materials see if they can write more animals on the Venn diagram.

⇨ *SEN support: Provide adult support for both the reading and information retrieval aspects of this activity. Encourage the children to look for key words (food, eating habits) in simple texts or by using ICT sources.*

⇨ *Extension: Challenge able children to consider alternative ways of recording this information (i.e. to devise a classification system), perhaps including other features of animals at the same time.*

Review – Encourage pupils to review their findings with another pair.

Transfer and compare

- Show the children a wide variety of PE equipment (this could be part of a PE lesson) and ask them how they would organise this equipment in the storage area so that it could be easily accessed for specific lessons (gymnastics, dance, team games etc.).

- Discuss the criteria that could be used (e.g. size, shape, frequency of use etc).

Thinking about thinking

Help pupils to assess the thinking skills they have used in this activity and, if time allows, record them in their Thinking Books.

Think-links

Encourage the children to transfer the thinking skills they have used in this activity to other areas of the curriculum. These could include:

Literacy – project-based enquiries;

Numeracy – use a range of data-collecting techniques;

Music – classify musical instruments or genres, using given criteria.

Thinking skills

Enqu	●
Prob	
Crea	
Info	●
Reas	
Eval	

Yes or No?

Main learning objectives: ask questions and decide how to find out answers; predict possible answers; select and record information.

Connect and prepare

1. As a class, talk about similarities and differences in the features of children in the class (e.g. hair colour, height, shoe size, eye colour etc.). Make a list of these ideas on the board.

2. Ask the children to decide yes or no in answer to the question 'Can children with the longest legs run the fastest?' The children may predict that the answer to this question is 'yes'. Then tell the class they are going to test their predictions. Discuss whether all the children in the class need to be checked or not – allow the children to decide, giving reasons for their decisions.

Think, do, review

Think – Ask the children to predict answers 'yes' or 'no' to the question: 'Do the tallest children have the largest shoe size?'.

Do – Encourage the children, working individually or in pairs, to test their predictions and choose a way of recording their findings.

⇨ **SEN support:** *Prompt SEN children with open-ended questions during the task and allow them to record pictorially.*

⇨ **Extension:** *Ask able pupils to think of and write down any other questions the class could investigate.*

Review – Discuss pupils' findings and the different ways they have been recorded.

Transfer and compare

● Ask the children to predict findings for some of the questions devised by the children undertaking the extension task. As a class ask the children to suggest enquiry methods and possible ways of recording their findings.

● Compare all three tasks (testing predictions, writing questions and thinking of enquiry methods) for skills and strategies used and ways of recording.

Thinking about thinking

Help pupils to assess the thinking skills they have used in this activity and, if time allows, record them in their Thinking Books.

Think-links

Encourage the children to transfer the thinking skills they have used in this activity to other curriculum areas. These could include:

Science – find different ways to solve problems by asking questions, predicting outcomes, testing conclusions and improving solutions;

History – ask questions to be investigated about what it was like to live at different times in the past;

ICT – use data-handling software to present findings in a range of formats;

PE – predict how long it takes to complete a variety of actions (e.g. running round the playground, or how many skips in a minute, etc.) and time them, then record the findings.

The Yeti – Does it Exist?

Many scientists all over the world do not believe there is such a thing as a yeti, or wildman. They believe that people have been:

- making up all the stories;
- making fake plaster-casts; and
- taking fake photos or films.

because:

(a) they want to sell their stories and earn a lot of money; or

(b) they want to become famous and see their pictures in the newspapers and on TV; or

(c) they want to play clever tricks on the scientists.

What do you think?

Look at this chart. It is partly filled in, but there are a lot of gaps. Then read the reports that claim yeti sightings. Each report has a number. Fill in the rest of the chart using the information in the reports.

Report	How tall?	Size of footprint	What colour?	Where seen?	When?
1					
2	2 m 40 cm				
3					1967
4					
5					
6		50 cm			
7					
8			black		

The Yeti – Does it Exist?

Reports of yeti sightings

1. In 1951 an explorer climbing Mount Everest saw a number of strange footprints. They did not look like anything he had ever seen before, so he took a photo of one of them, with his ice-axe beside it to show how big it was. The footprint measured 33 centimetres long and 20 centimetres wide. It had two big toes and two small ones.

2. One night in Canada, in 1924, a traveller was sleeping in his tent. He was woken up in the middle of the night by something picking him up and carrying him, in his sleeping-bag. After a very long journey he was put down on the ground. When he looked up he saw a family of four hairy creatures who looked rather like people. The man creature was about 2 metres 40 centimetres tall. The traveller fired a shot from his rifle, which he had with him in his sleeping-bag, and the creatures ran away.

3. In 1967, two Americans saw what they thought was a female yeti and they took some film of her turning round to walk away. When she had gone they measured her footprints and worked out that she must have been about 2 metres 15 centimetres tall. Many scientists don't believe this story. They say that the film was made up. But others think it could be true.

4. In 1969 a giant dead 'apeman', in a block of ice, was taken around America by people who said that its body had been found in the jungle in Vietnam. A local woman had been attacked by it and she had shot it in the head. Many people who saw it thought it was a rubber model made to look like a yeti. But two scientists examined the body and announced that it was real. They thought it was a Neanderthal man, like the ape-men who lived on our planet thousands of years ago. Some people did not believe this story, and the body in ice has since disappeared.

5. In 1958 a Russian scientist said he caught sight of a yeti coming out of a cave near the top of a cliff. He described the creature as long armed and covered in reddish-grey hair. When he asked people in the village nearby, they told him that they had seen this creature too and they called it 'the wild man'.

6. In 1981, in Russia, some scientists looking for the yeti discovered one enormous footprint. They made a plaster-cast of it. It measured 50 centimetres long.

7. In 1983 two women camping in the Himalayas reported seeing a female wildman, sitting on a rock 9 metres from their tent. It watched them for a long time, making munching sounds. They did not dare to approach it, and in the morning it had gone. They could not find any footprints or hairs.

8. In 1981, a shepherd drove his sheep back down from the mountains two months early. He said it was because he seen a big black wildman near his pasture. It had frightened his dogs and he did not dare stay there any longer. Since then, shepherds always work in pairs so that no one needs to stay alone in the mountains again at night.

Ly	●
Ny	
Sc	○
ICT	○
RE	>
Hi	○
Gg	○
DT	
AD	
Mu	
PE	
PSHE	

Thinking skills

Enqu	
Prob	
Crea	
Info	●
Reas	●
Eval	

The Yeti – Does it Exist?

Main learning objectives: use evidence to support reasoning; recognise that conclusions may draw on both implicit and explicit evidence.

Connect and prepare

1. Ask the children if they have heard of the yeti and what they know about it.
2. Talk about the different kinds of evidence that exist and how reliable they might be (e.g. witness accounts, photos etc.).

Think, do, review

Hand out copies of the activity sheet.

Think – Ask/help the children to read the instructions, define the task and think about the strategies they will need to use to complete the task. Make sure they read one report at a time and extract from it any relevant information to fill in the chart.

Do – Pupils should fill in the chart, using the written evidence to help them.

⇨ **SEN support:** *Provide adult support for the reading part of the activity.*

⇨ **Extension:** *Challenge able children to find out about other mysteries (e.g. the Bermuda Triangle or the Marie Celeste).*

Review – Talk about the evidence with the class. For example:

– Are there any pieces of evidence that appear more persuasive than others? Do you believe them all? Does the evidence convince you that the yeti exists?

Ask the class to vote whether they believe that the yeti exists, based on reading the evidence.

Transfer and compare

Show the class a photo of the Loch Ness Monster and talk about using photos as evidence. Compare photographic evidence with that of eye witness accounts. Which is more convincing?

Thinking about thinking

Help pupils to assess the thinking skills they have used in this activity and, if time allows, record them in their Thinking Books.

Think-links

Encourage the children to transfer the thinking skills they have used in this activity to other areas of the curriculum, such as:

Literacy – compile character profiles from evidence in the text;

Science – research and classify facts about animals, plants or materials;

RE – research and classify features of different faiths or ceremonies;

History – use a range of sources (artefacts, paintings, photos and writings) to investigate, record and classify information about life in the past.

A Week at School

Timetable 1

	Monday	Tuesday	Wednesday	Thursday	Friday
9.00–10.00	Numeracy	Numeracy	Literacy	Numeracy	Numeracy
10.00–10.15	Assembly	Assembly	Assembly	Assembly	Assembly
10.15–10.30	B	R	E	A	K
10.30–11.30	Literacy	Literacy	PE	Literacy	Literacy
11.30–12.30	Music	ICT	French	ICT	PSHE
			PSHE		Singing
12.30–1.30	L	U	N	C	H
1.30–2.30	PE	History	Numeracy	DT	Science
2.30–3.30	Science	Art	Geography	RE	Golden Time

© Jacquie Buttriss and Ann Callander (2005) *Think About It!*, David Fulton Publishers Ltd.

A Week at School

Timetable 2

	Monday	Tuesday	Wednesday	Thursday	Friday
9.00–10.00					
10.00–10.15					
10.15–10.30	B	R	E	A	K
10.30–11.30					
11.30–12.30					
12.30–1.30	L	U	N	C	H
1.30–2.30					
2.30–3.30					

A Week at School

Curriculum coverage

Ly	>
Ny	●
Sc	>
ICT	>
RE	
Hi	
Gg	>
DT	
AD	
Mu	
PE	
PSHE	○

Thinking skills

Enqu	
Prob	
Crea	●
Info	●
Reas	
Eval	

Main learning objectives: to locate relevant information, organise information using a given format and suggest alternative ideas.

Connect and prepare

1. Ask the children to talk about the different kinds of charts they have used to find out or convey information. Discuss similarities and differences.

2. Ask the children to look at the timetable of Class 6's week at school on activity sheet A. How different is this from their own class timetable? Together, analyse the information that Class 6's timetable gives (e.g. look at how often and for how long Class 6 studies each subject; which subject do they study most/least?). Record key information as a class with an adult scribing on the board.

Think, do, review

Think – Ask the children to think about the lessons they would most like to have during a week, as well as those they feel they need.

Do – Ask the pupils, working in pairs, to plan a week for their class and show this on the blank timetable on activity sheet B.

⇨ **SEN support:** *Prior discussion (with adult) to clarify ideas (e.g. what subjects, when and how often). The use of colour coding for each subject area could help some children.*

⇨ **Extension:** *Challenge able pupils to think of other lessons or activities they would like to add to the week and give reasons for their inclusion. They could also consider designing their own timetable format with different timings and rationale.*

Review – Each pair of children should share and discuss their proposed timetables with other pairs.

Transfer and compare

● As a class, look at some of the timetables the children have produced and talk about the variety (or lack of variety) of lessons included. Discuss the similarities and differences between the children's weekly plans and Class 6's week at school.

● Have a vote about which is the most popular lesson or activity in the week.

Thinking about thinking

Help pupils to assess the thinking skills they have used in this activity and, if time allows, record them in their Thinking Books.

Think-links

Encourage the children to transfer the thinking skills they have used in this activity to other areas of the curriculum, such as:

Literacy – retrieve and interpret information from charts and diagrams and explain findings in narrative form;

ICT – construct charts and graphs related to projects;

Science – construct charts to show data from test results;

Geography – compile and interpret weather charts.

Promises

Long ago, in Japan, there lived a poor, young fisherman. His name was Urashima. He lived with his mother in a small house by the sea. Every day he went fishing and caught enough fish for them to eat. Every day he promised his mother that he would do his best to return home safely in the evening.

One day, as he set off with his fishing pole, he saw some children throwing stones at a small turtle. Urashima felt sorry for the turtle and chased the children away. Then he put the turtle back into the water and it swam out into the sea.

The next day, when Urashima went fishing, a large turtle appeared in the water. It was the same turtle that Urashima had rescued the day before but now it was much larger. 'Climb on my back,' said the turtle. 'I will show you many wonderful things below the sea.'

Urashima forgot the promise he had made to his mother. He climbed on the turtle's back and went with him to a kingdom far below the sea. The turtle took Urashima to the palace of the sea-king. There he was treated like a rich man. He was given everything he could wish for and more.

After a while Urashima began to miss his old life back on dry land. The daughter of the sea-king wanted him to stay but Urashima was determined to return home. At last she agreed and handed him a small box. 'When you return home you must take this box,' she said. 'The turtle will come for you if you hold this box and wish. But you must never open it if you want to visit us again.'

Urashima promised not to open the box and the turtle took him back to dry land. But as Urashima walked along the sandy path to his village, he noticed that everything looked different. He walked until he came to his house. But the house was empty. No one lived there any more. Sadly Urashima walked along the path until he saw an old man.

'Where is the woman who lived in that house?' Urashima asked.

'She died many years ago,' replied the old man. 'Her son went fishing and promised to return, but he never did.'

Urashima was puzzled. He did not think that he had been away for so long. He walked back to the seashore and sat on a rock. He looked at the box that the sea-princess had given him. 'Perhaps I will find the answer inside the box,' he thought. Urashima forgot about his promise and opened the box. But there was nothing inside.

Urashima felt sad as he sat on the rock and looked out to sea. He called to the turtle, but it did not come. He looked down into the rock pool and saw his face. It was the face of an old man. He looked at his hands. They were the hands of an old man.

Then Urashima realised that time under the sea was different from time on dry land. But broken promises are the same wherever you are.

Promises

Character profile

Name:

Age:

Occupation:

Family:

Country of birth:

Home:

Appearance:

Likes:

Dislikes:

Ambitions:

Personality:

Promises

Curriculum coverage

Ly	●
Ny	
Sc	
ICT	
RE	>
Hi	>
Gg	
DT	
AD	○
Mu	
PE	
PSHE	●

Main learning objectives: use literal and inferential comprehension to make deductions about a character; use explicit and implicit evidence to draw conclusions.

Connect and prepare

1. Introduce the activity to the children by talking about the meaning of the word 'promise'.

2. Ask the children, working in pairs, to role play an everyday situation where a promise is made and broken. Then, discuss the possible outcomes of some of these situations.

3. Read the story 'Promises' aloud from activity sheet A. Discuss the meaning of the last two sentences.

4. Ask the children to brainstorm ideas about what may have been inside the box (write these ideas on the board as a word web or mind map). Show the children's ideas visually and encourage them to identify ideas that link.

Thinking skills

Enqu	
Prob	
Crea	
Info	
Reas	●
Eval	●

Think, do, review

Think – Encourage the children to think about Urashima as a person and what they have learnt about him so far.

Do – Ask the children to compile the character profile for Urashima using activity sheet B. Children should have a copy of the text on activity sheet A to share. The aim of this activity is to use both literal and inferential evidence from the text to compile a thoughtful character profile.

⇨ *SEN support: Adult support may be needed to compile as much of the character profile as the children understand, using pause, prompt and praise techniques.*

⇨ *Extension: 'Promises' is a traditional story from Japan. Most countries have their own traditional stories and many of these have a message or moral. Challenge able children to find other traditional stories with messages or morals and compare them with 'Promises'.*

Review – Ask the children to compare their character profiles with others in small groups and review the evidence for their thoughts and ideas.

Transfer and compare

As a class, compile a character profile after looking carefully at a portrait. Compare this task with the previous task of compiling a character profile from a text.

Thinking about thinking

Help pupils to assess the thinking skills they have used in this activity and, if time allows, record them in their Thinking Books.

Think-links

Encourage the children to transfer the thinking skills they have used in this activity to other areas of the curriculum, such as:

Literacy – compile character profiles using evidence from texts; role play specific characters and situations related to a story;

History – use different types of historical evidence to help form opinions about characters in history;

Art and design – use clues in portraits to find out more about a person;

RE – use religious writings to help understand people and their ways of life, both now and in the past.

Family Tree

Rosie's family

Here is Rosie's family tree, showing everyone's name.

- ● = means that these two people are married to each other.
- ● b. means the dates when people were born
- ● Names in capital letters are the surnames which do not change.
- ● Names in brackets are the surnames people change from when they get married. (For example, when James and Anne were married they became James and Ann Rose.)

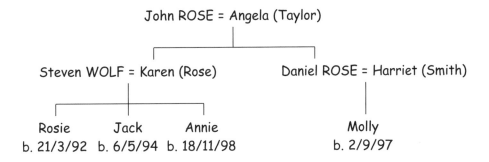

Here is the same family tree, but this time it shows all the people's relationships to Rosie.

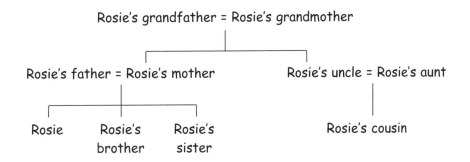

Other relationship words

niece	nephew	granddaughter	grandson
son-in-law	daughter-in-law	mother-in-law	father-in-law
	sister-in-law	brother-in-law	

Family Tree

Question 1–10

Fill in the gaps about Rosie's family:

1. Karen is Molly's ....

2. Molly is Jack's ....

3. Harriet changed her surname to .... when she got married.

4. Jack is John's ....

5. .... is John's eldest grandchild.

6. Steven is Karen's ....

7. Harriet is Angela's ....

8. Jack is Daniel's ....

9. Molly is Karen's ....

10. Daniel is Annie's ....

Questions 11–15

11. Who is Harriet's nephew?

12. Who is Angela's son-in-law?

13. Who is Angela and John's youngest grandchild?

14. Who is Molly's eldest cousin?

15. What was Karen's surname after her marriage?

Extension questions 16–18

16. Who is John's daughter-in-law?

17. Molly shows a photo to her friend, saying 'This boy is my uncle's son.' What is the boy's name?

18. Rosie shows her teacher a photo and says this girl is now grown up. Her daughter is my mother's niece. Who is the girl in the photo?

Family Tree

Joe's family

Read the following paragraph and fill in the family tree.
(Hint: Use a pencil, so that you can rub out any mistakes.)

Joe is the youngest son of Don and Susie White. Joe has an eight-year-old sister called Zoe and a five-year-old brother called Billy. Don is the older child of David and Val White. Don's younger sister is called Alison and she is married to Chris Stewart. Alison and Chris have one child called Finlay, who is still a baby.

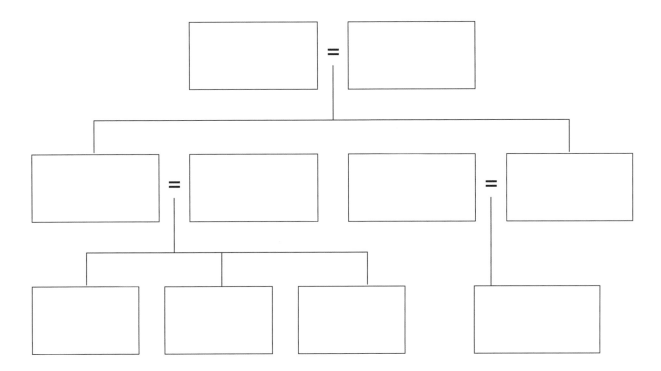

Curriculum
coverage

Ly	○
Ny	
Sc	
ICT	
RE	>
Hi	●
Gg	
DT	
AD	
Mu	
PE	
PSHE	>

Thinking skills

Enqu	●
Prob	
Crea	
Info	●
Reas	
Eval	

Family Tree

Main learning objectives: to learn how to analyse and evaluate information; to show relationships in diagrammatic form.

Connect and prepare

1. As a class, list all the different relations children can think of (e.g. aunt, cousin). Talk about how they relate to each other (e.g. if you are a man's niece, what is he to you?).

2. Explain and show what a family tree looks like using Rosie's family on activity sheet A. Explain that the equals symbol means 'married' and how women often change their names when they get married.

3. Go through Rosie's family tree with the class, discussing the various relationships.

Think, do, review

Think – Ask the children, working in small groups, to look through Rosie's family tree again together with the relationships tree, and ask them to discuss how the relationships have been worked out. Discuss the new relationship words shown at the bottom of the sheet.

⇨ *SEN support: Help SEN pupils by prompting and guiding them as appropriate.*

⇨ *Extension: Challenge able pupils to write one sentence to explain what each new relationship word means.*

Do – Ask the children to look at the sentences about Rosie's family tree on activity sheet B and work together, as a whole class, to fill in the gaps in numbers 1 to 10. Then ask the children to work on their own or in pairs to answer questions 11 to 15.

⇨ *Extension: Able pupils who could do this on their own, at a faster pace, can move on to questions 16 to 18.*

Review – Ask the children, as a class or in pairs/groups, to discuss: How did you do this task? How successful was it? Could you have done it a different/better way?

Transfer and compare

● Ask the pupils, in pairs, to read through the paragraph about Joe's family tree on activity sheet C and write the names in the appropriate boxes.

⇨ *SEN support: Provide SEN pupils with adult help, leading them through the task.*

⇨ *Extension: Challenge able pupils to see if they can make up some questions like questions 17 and 18 about this new family and test them out on each other (or the teacher).*

- Ask the children to discuss how they did this task – did the previous task about Rosie's family help them?

Thinking about thinking

Help pupils to assess the thinking skills they have used in this activity and, if time allows, record them in their Thinking Books.

Think-links

Encourage pupils to transfer their learning to show relationships across the curriculum:

Literacy – use family trees to portray relationships in stories;

History – show the relationships of historical characters (e.g. monarchy);

RE – use family trees for relationships in the Bible or in other religious books/stories;

PSHE – encourage pupils to draw their own family trees (perhaps for homework).

Curriculum
coverage

Ly	>
Ny	
Sc	
ICT	>
RE	
Hi	
Gg	
DT	
AD	●
Mu	>
PE	●
PSHE	○

Thinking skills

Enqu	
Prob	
Crea	●
Info	
Reas	●
Eval	

Sports Day

Main learning objective: Look at and think about things from different points of view and reflect critically on ideas, explaining reasons for choices.

Connect and prepare

Tell the children that your school has been asked to put together a collection of artwork, showing what sports day means to everyone. (You could involve a governor in this.) Ask the following questions:
– Who do you think 'everyone' means? (i.e. Who is everyone?)
– What do you think is special about this school's sports day? (i.e. What are the key events, themes, ethos?)
– Who is it for – pupils, parents, staff, visitors?

Think, do, review

Think – Ask the class to think about what kind of scenes would be best to show what goes on at this school's sports day. Discuss their responses and note the key ideas on the board.
Do – Pupils do their artwork. These can be paintings, collages, prints or sculptures.

⇨ *Extension: Able pupils should consider whose point(s) of view they are portraying and how best to show feelings in their pictures (e.g. expressions, body language, etc.).*

Review – In groups, or as a whole class, encourage the pupils to look at all their artwork and ask/answer:
– Do they show a range of different things about sports day?
– Do they give an outsider a clear idea of what our sports day is like?
Pick one picture to talk about in more detail and discuss feelings and points of view.

Transfer and compare

● Now, as a class, sort all the pieces of artwork into groups (e.g. those showing individuals, groups, activities/races, spectators, whole scenes).

● As a class, select six pieces of artwork to include at your school's exhibition. The children must say why they think each one should be included – these six pieces of artwork should show what sports day *means* to everyone, rather than just be the ones that look good.)

Thinking about thinking

Help pupils to assess the thinking skills they have used in this activity and, if time allows, record them in their Thinking Books.

Think-links

Encourage the children to think about other subjects in the curriculum where they could express different points of view, such as:

Literacy – encourage pupils in their choice of appropriate vocabulary to express feelings and 'paint' moods;

Music – portray ethos, moods or feelings through musical composition and performance;

Drama – pupils can use role-play to convey feelings and moods;

ICT – ask pupils to use a graphics program to represent scenes in particular ways;

PSHE – use circle times to encourage discussion about different points of view.

The Challenge of King Minos

A long time ago, on the island of Crete, there lived a powerful king. His name was King Minos and he was cruel as well as powerful. Every year he sent for seven young men and seven young women from the mainland of Greece to take part in a sport called bull-leaping. This was a dangerous sport and many of the young men and women were killed by the bulls. Some tried to escape from the island in small boats, so the king decided to build a special underground maze where he could keep his prisoners. Among King Minos's prisoners was a man called Daedalus. He was a clever designer and inventor and, with his son Icarus, had built some useful inventions for King Minos.

King Minos challenged Daedalus to design a maze that would be so complicated that no one would be able to escape. In the centre of the maze he asked Daedalus to design a special room where a strange creature called the Minotaur could live. The Minotaur was half man and half bull and would catch any prisoners who tried to escape. Daedalus had to work out a complicated design before the underground maze could be built.

Escape!

Daedalus and his son Icarus were not kept in the maze. They were allowed to move freely about the island, but they were not allowed to leave the island of Crete. King Minos wanted to keep them because they were so clever at designing things. But Daedalus did manage to escape. How do you think he escaped? Can you design a way of escaping?

© Jacquie Buttriss and Ann Callander (2005) *Think About It!*, David Fulton Publishers Ltd.

The Challenge of King Minos

Curriculum coverage

Ly	●
Ny	>
Sc	
ICT	>
RE	
Hi	
Gg	>
DT	●
AD	>
Mu	
PE	
PSHE	

Main learning objectives: to try different ways of responding to a design challenge, develop creative ideas and evaluate effectiveness of designs using given criteria.

Connect and prepare

1. As a class discuss with the children their experiences of mazes, both garden mazes and puzzle book mazes.

2. Discuss different maze shapes.

3. Hand out copies of the activity sheet and together read the challenge that King Minos gave to Daedalus (the first two paragraphs).

Think, do, review

Think – Ask the children to think of different ways in which they could design a maze for King Minos, making it as complicated as possible.

Do – Ask the children to design mazes using different shapes.

⇨ *SEN support: Ensure that children have tools and materials to help them with the task (some may prefer rulers, some shapes to draw round etc.).*

⇨ *Extension: Challenge able children to try out different shapes and decide on which might result in the most interesting or complex maze.*

Review – Children should review their designs with a partner and decide on the levels of complexity of their mazes.

Thinking skills

Enqu	
Prob	●
Crea	●
Info	
Reas	
Eval	●

Transfer and compare

- Ask the children to read 'Escape!' and sketch a draft design, showing their ideas for ways of escaping from the maze.

- Ask the children to discuss whether this activity (devising an escape plan) was more or less difficult than designing a maze, giving reasons for their answers.

Thinking about thinking

Help pupils to assess the thinking skills they have used in this activity and, if time allows, record them in their Thinking Books.

Think-links

Encourage the children to transfer the thinking skills they have used in this activity to other curriculum areas, such as:

Numeracy – create reflective symmetry designs, using 2D shapes;

ICT – devise a simple maze that you can lay out with wooden bricks on the floor and direct a programmable robot through it;

Geography – identify an area of the school environment in need of redesigning and suggest possible ideas;

Art and design – Design posters for school events or covers for project folders.

Holiday Races
Teacher's guide

Connect and prepare

In preparation for this activity draw this simple diagram of three blank cells on the board.

Now draw this grid below it. (You could draw the shapes and use colour pens to signify the colours.)

	square	triangle	circle	left	middle	right
blue						
green						
red						
left						
middle						
right						

Write up the statements on the board nearby:

- There are three shapes in a row in the top diagram.
- The blue shape is on the left.
- The square is green.
- The shape with three sides is on the right.
- The circle is not red.

Now help pupils to fill in the grid. *NB* You will need to demonstrate to the class that when you put in a tick in response to a statement, straight away you can put in crosses in the other cells in the same column and the same row of that section. For example, 'the blue shape is on the left' – it therefore can't be in the middle or on the right and, similarly, neither of the other colours can be on the left (see the completed grid below).

The completed grid and diagram

This is how the grid and diagram should look when the task is complete.

blue square	circle red	green triangle

	square	triangle	circle	left	middle	right
blue	X	X	✓	✓	X	X
green	✓	X	X	X	✓	X
red	X	✓	X	X	X	✓
left	X	X	✓			
middle	✓	X	X			
right	X	✓	X			

Solutions to activity sheets A and B

Sheet A – **1st** Ali in white; **2nd** Sarah in blue; **3rd** Dan in green; **4th** Gemma in red.

Sheet B – **lane 1** Ben with curly hair; **lane 2** Sally with a pony-tail; **lane 3** Greg with spiky hair; **lane 4** Jack with a long fringe; **lane 5** Kate with braids.

Holiday Races

1st	2nd	3rd	4th

There were four children in a race. They each wore different colours.

- The boy in green came third.
- The winner was a boy wearing white.
- Sarah finished ahead of Dan.
- The girl in red came last.

Can you work out the order in which they all finished?

Use this grid to help you work it all out.

	1st	2nd	3rd	4th	green	white	red	blue
Sarah								
Gemma								
Dan								
Ali								
green								
white								
red								
blue								

When you have worked out the answers, write the children's names and the colours they were wearing in the diagram at the top of this page.

Holiday Races

Lane 1	Lane 2	Lane 3	Lane 4	Lane 5

Five children were lining up for a race on the beach. Each of them had different hair-styles.

- Greg has spiky hair.
- Jack is standing between Greg and Kate.
- A boy is in lane 1.
- The person with a long fringe is in lane 4.
- Sally is not in an end lane.
- The person in lane 2 has a pony tail.
- Ben has curly hair.
- Kate is in an end lane.

Can you work out which lane each of them is in?

Use this grid to help you work it all out.

	1	2	3	4	5	braids	curly hair	long fringe	pony tail	spiky hair
Greg										
Ben										
Jack										
Sally										
Kate										
braids										
curly hair										
long fringe										
pony tail										
spiky hair										

When you have worked out the answers, write the children's names and hair-styles in their lanes in the diagram at the top of this page.

Holiday Races

Curriculum
coverage

Ly	
Ny	●
Sc	>
ICT	>
RE	
Hi	>
Gg	>
DT	
AD	
Mu	
PE	
PSHE	

Main learning objective: Sort and classify relevant information using a given structure, explaining what they have done and why.

Connect and prepare

1. Ask the children to explain the meaning of the word 'grid'. Explore different meanings/contexts. Has anyone used a grid before to help sort out information? (If so, find out what they used it for and how they used it.)

2. Using the material you have copied on to the board from the Teacher's guide ask the class to help you fill in the grid. When it is finished, ask individuals to come up and draw the coloured shapes in the appropriate cells of the simple diagram. (See the Teacher's guide for how the grid and diagram should look when the task is complete.)

Think, do, review

Thinking skills

Enqu	
Prob	
Crea	
Info	●
Reas	●
Eval	

Think – Ask the pupils to think about what skills they needed to use to complete this grid. What would have made it harder? Together as a class, make up another example on the board, using a larger grid and trying to make it more difficult.
Do – Now give out 'Holiday Races' activity sheet A and ask the children to read the information with a partner.

⇨ *SEN support: Assist pupils by reading it out for or with them.*

⇨ *Extension: Challenge more able pupils to tackle activity sheet B instead of A. They should complete this more complex task on their own (not with a partner).*

Stop and ask them what they think they have to do. They should now complete the task with their partner, each filling in their own grid and discussing their progress.
Review – As a class, compare solutions and discuss how the children tackled the task. Encourage them to explain what was difficult as well as what was easy.

Transfer and compare

Now ask pupils, working in pairs, to make up their own simple grids about pets and prepare statements to go with them, trying them out to make sure they work.

⇨ *SEN support: Assist SEN pupils by providing adult help or some simple guidelines.*

⇨ *Extension: Challenge able pupils to do this task individually and build in another layer of attributes if they wish, making the grids more complex.*

Thinking about thinking

Help pupils to assess the thinking skills they have used in this activity and, if time allows, record them in their Thinking Books.

Think-links

Encourage pupils to think of areas of the curriculum where grids like these could be used:

Science – sorting and classifying information or findings;

Geography – sorting and classifying features and/or identifying locations;

History – collating information about historical events;

ICT – dragging items into their correct positions as part of a computer simulation.

References

DfES (2004) *Excellence and Enjoyment: Learning and Teaching in the Primary Years. Learning to learn: progression in key aspects of learning,* September, Ref: DfES 0524-2004G., p. 12.

DfES/QCA (2000) *National Curriculum: Handbook for Primary Teachers in England – Key Stages 1 and 2.*

QCA *Guidance on Teaching the Gifted and Talented – Managing Provision.* www.nc.uk.net/gt